380

Morality and Modern Warfare

edited by William J. Nagle

THE STATE OF THE QUESTION

Morality
and
Modern Warfare

Baltimore
HELICON PRESS
1960

acknowledgments

THE EDITOR is grateful to *Theology Digest* for permission to reprint the articles by Fathers John C. Ford, S.J. and John R. Connery, S.J., and to the Catholic Association for International Peace for permission to use the addresses of Mr. Thomas E. Murray and Father John Courtney Murray, S.J., which were originally delivered at meetings of that organization.

Prof. William V. O'Brien provided the impetus that got the symposium underway. Professor O'Brien's own studies at Georgetown University's Institute of World Polity on the international law of war and other subjects related to morality and warfare have served as a constant source of stimulation to me, and I gratefully acknowledge my debt to him.

Thanks to the excellent cooperation of the contributors, this volume is truly a symposium. Although working under tight deadlines, the writers read the drafts of each other's articles and commented on them. Whenever possible, discussions between the contributors were arranged. The reader will note the frequency with which an author refers specifically to points made elsewhere in the symposium. The editor is especially appreciative of the constant help he received from one of the contributors, Col. John K. Moriarty.

The select bibliography on morality and warfare, which serves as the final contribution to the symposium, is in large part a product of Georgetown's Institute of World Polity. It was as a research assistant at the Institute that Noel J. Brown undertook the compilation of titles; Jean-Robert Leguey-Feilleux, senior research assistant at the Institute, devoted many additional hours to the exacting task. Suggestions for titles were solicited from many scholars here and abroad; Professors R. Paul Ramsey, Ernst F. Winter and E. A. Conway, S.J., deserve particular mention for their kind assistance on the bibliography.

Friends who gave generously of their time and talents in reading the various selections and in making suggestions on them include Professors Heinrich A. Rommen, Ulrich S. Allers and Henry B. Cushing, Dean C. J. Nuesse, Fathers E. A. Conway, S.J., and Robert W. Hovda, William J. Kerrigan, Jeane J. Kirkpatrick, and Richard T. Greer. I am deeply grateful also for the help and encouragement I received from Margaret C. Stigers, Lillian Perkins, Constance L. Pierson, and, especially, from my wife, Patricia.

WILLIAM J. NAGLE

contents

Morality and Modern Warfare

chapter I

Introduction

by William J. Nagle

THAT THE publication of this symposium[1] on morality and warfare has the character of a pioneer effort fifteen years after Hiroshima indicates something of the failure of the Christian community to come to terms with that event. The moral confusion that this failure evidences may be but a part of the general state of shock the public has invoked as a psychological defense against the horrors of modern warfare. Many desire neither to hear about these realities nor to think about them.

A very few people have tried in the last decade to shake us from our apathy. Their reward was frustration. Thomas E. Murray, in his years on the Atomic Energy Commission, worked to build an informed and morally conscious public opinion on atomic energy and warfare. In May, 1957, he wrote an article for *Life* magazine. To demonstrate what he felt to be the absurdity of all-out war, he posited

[1] The essays by Dougherty, Moriarty, Zahn and O'Brien, as well as Mr. Brown's bibliography, were prepared specifically for this symposium; the articles by T. E. Murray, Connery, Ford and J. C. Murray have appeared elsewhere.

3

the explosion of 3500 megatons of fission energy — the equivalent of 3,500,000,000 tons of TNT — in a war between the United States and the Soviet Union. He then calculated the results in terms of strontium-90, the cancer producing by-product of an atomic explosion. He estimated that in the Soviet Union and the United States the strontium level in human bones would be 50 times the maximum considered acceptable for general populations. World-wide fallout from the explosion would produce strontium concentrations that would be between two and six times this maximum. This was one of the most startling statements made by a prominent government official on the consequences of all-out war. For all the response it evoked, Mr. Murray might as well have devoted his efforts to calculating the number of people who would consume tranquilizers in the crisis.

The tradition that even war must be limited by the norms of justice is breaking down. Mr. Murray, in his contribution to this symposium, refers to the rupture of the Christian tradition of a "civilized" warfare. He cites the obliteration bombing of World War II, the atomic bombing of Hiroshima and Nagasaki, and the notions of total victory and unconditional surrender as indications that the tradition of civilized warfare has been replaced by the doctrine of total war. This abandonment of the civilized tradition has gone largely uncriticized and unopposed by the religious-minded people of our country.

It may be that the Christian's acute awareness of the evils of totalitarianism makes him reluctant to judge the morality of the means used to oppose it. If this be so, Christopher Dawson's warning of a malady which he calls the "indifference of means" is relevant. He describes it as "the new evil that has spread from Russia into the heart of Europe. It is no longer necessarily associated with communism. On the contrary, it spreads by opposition, even more than by imitation. As soon as men decide that all means are permitted to fight an evil, then their good becomes indistinguishable from the evil that they set out to destroy."

There are individuals and organizations in the United States that do not deserve the adjective "apathetic." The names of Reinhold Niebuhr, Paul Ramsey, Kenneth W. Thompson, William Lee Miller,

John C. Bennett, and Ernest W. Lefever among the Protestant writers and Robert Gordis and Arthur A. Cohen among the Jewish writers come readily to mind. Father E. A. Conway, S.J., is widely and justly acclaimed for his knowledge of the complexities of disarmament and related problems. Robert Hoyt, John Cogley and Donald McDonald must be numbered among the Catholic writers who have tried to dispel the mist of apathy that surrounds the question of morality and warfare. The interdenominational Church Peace Union and its publication *Worldview*, under the editorship of William Clancy, has probably done more than any other single organization or institution in the United States to stimulate study and discussion of the problems of morality and war. The CAIP (Catholic Association for International Peace) has also evidenced concern. Two of the contributions to this present volume were first given as addresses at meetings of the CAIP; most of the contributors to this book are members of that organization.

All the contributors are Catholics living in the United States. In one sense such a restriction needs no defense; each of the writers is a competent scholar with a knowledge of his subject that would be welcome in any discussion under any auspices. That the editor and publisher limited the symposium to Catholic contributors consciously and deliberately may require some explanation. The restriction carries with it no implication that the writings of the Protestant or Jewish thinkers listed above are somehow less relevant than the work of Catholic scholars. Many of the writings of these men, however, have already been made widely available to the reading public. Catholics in the United States have not been as articulate; [2] thus the desire to stimulate other Catholic scholars to address themselves to the problem of morality and warfare was a primary motivation for this book. The morality of modern warfare is not a question on which American members of the largest unified religious group within

[2] The experience of Mr. Noel J. Brown in preparing the bibliography for this volume substantiates a report made by Fr. L. C. McHugh, S.J., of *America* magazine. Remarking on the dearth of moral discourse on war, Fr. McHugh noted that out of the 56,176 items in the *Catholic Periodical Index* for the period June, 1954, to May, 1956, "the moral aspects of war rated four items; the moral aspects of atomic war rated eighteen items."

Christian civilization can remain silent; nor would their continued apathy be in keeping with a tradition that has produced Suárez, Vitoria, and other moral theorists on war. It is precisely the fact that the contributors to this volume — lay or clerical — are writing in the mainstream of that moral tradition that lends to their reflections special import for other Americans.

But it should be made quite clear that none of the contributors is writing as an official representative of the Catholic Church. The reader interested in the Church's generalized, "official" moral theory on war will find it succinctly summarized in part of Fr. Murray's article; beyond that the reader may be impressed and dismayed by the wide diversity of views expressed.

The variance of thought on this still "open-ended" theological question would have appeared even more noticeable had the volume included some of the work being done in Great Britain and in continental Europe. Last year there was published in Britain a book — titled *Morals and Missiles: Catholic Essays on the Problem of War Today*.[3] In comparing the essays in the British book with those in this symposium, one is struck by the strongly pacifist tone of the former. By contrast only one of the contributors to this U.S. symposium would term himself a pacifist.[4]

The difference provokes some rather interesting speculation. There is a possible relevancy in the fact that as Americans the contributors to this volume are citizens of the nation which has the major responsibility for the defense of the free world. The question here is not one of patriotism, but of responsibility. Were the contributors to the British volume living in the United States (and available,

[3] This worthwhile book (London: James Clarke Co., 1959) should find many interested readers in the U.S.; edited by Charles S. Thompson, with an introduction by Michael de la Bedoyere, it includes essays by such eminent spokesmen as Canon F. H. Drinkwater, Dom Bede Griffiths, O.S.B., Christopher Hollis, Sir Compton Mackenzie, Archbishop Thomas D. Roberts, S.J., Father Franziskus Stratmann, O.P., and E. I. Watkin.

[4] The comparison is valid, of course, only if this volume is truly representative of U.S. Catholic scholarship and if *Morals and Missiles* is representative of Catholic writing in Britain and continental Europe. With regard to the proportion between articulate pacifists and other Catholic writers in the United States, the editor is convinced that *Morality and Modern Warfare* reflects a fair representation.

say, as counselors to defense department officials), would their writings on war take on a different tone? Conversely, if the U.S. contributors had lived through the "blitz" and now found themselves on a little island under the shadow of multimegaton H-bombs, would their writings focus on different urgencies? This is not to suggest that the American writers are unconcerned about the physical and moral effects of any modern war; nor is it to imply that the British writers are ignoring the communist threat. It is only to say that the facts, the circumstances against which their respective moral positions are assumed, are not quite the same. Perhaps one may also see in this a partial explanation for the general unanimity between the few American Catholics and Protestants who have written on the problem.

Prof. Dougherty reminds us of the "brutal fact" that where the communist system triumphs, a new purely materialistic interpretation of the meaning of life on earth is substituted. "Western governments may deserve criticism for the form in which they have cast their defense policies," he writes, "but not for their preoccupation with the problem itself."

It might be easier to satisfy the demands of charity regarding warfare if one's responsibilities did not require the simultaneous consideration of obligations in justice regarding the spread of communism. In Bishop John J. Wright's eloquent appraisal of the two virtues at the 1958 meeting of the CAIP, he said "it is unfortunately not yet possible for honest theologians to deny that justice may require of us duties from which charity would prefer to shrink." He asserted that it is overemphasis of charity and neglect of justice that promotes pacifism. The need to balance the demands of *both* justice and charity is what poses the terrible moral dilemma of our day.

Yet it might be argued with some justification that however necessary the balance of justice and charity in the society as a whole, the balance need not exist to the same degree in the individual person. A balance of conservative and liberal elements is needed for a stable, well-ordered political society, but they need not exist in comparable measure in each citizen. Many more Gordon Zahns and Dorothy Days might be welcomed on the American scene, not for the help

7

they will give in solving the dilemma, but for prodding our consciences and forcing the rest of us to come to terms with the problem.

There is a further point. The military strategy of the West is largely determined by the United States. If that strategy is to be brought more closely into line with the demands of morality, it will most likely be done, not in London, Paris or The Hague, but in Washington. And it will be done not as a consequence of the demands of religiously-oriented people in Britain, France or Holland but because American citizens with correctly-formed consciences have affected U.S. policy-makers and strategists. What clearly emerges is the strong obligation of those U.S. citizens who profess to be moral creatures to begin to form correct consciences of their own on war.

The job of forming a correct conscience on modern warfare is not an easy task, given the extreme complexity of the problem. Mr. Murray, in a 1958 address at the Catholic University of America on public opinion and the problem of war, noted the "enormously increased complexity of public affairs, in themselves and in the manner in which they put problems to the Christian conscience." He went on to say that today the premium is on wide and accurate knowledge, "since what has to be done will become clear, if at all, only after serious study."

This point is one of the underlying themes of this symposium. It finds most succinct expression in Fr. Murray's plea for a "vigorous cultivation of politico-moral science." Prof. Dougherty echoes the call when he urges that our arguments on defense policy be advanced "not only on the grounds of what constitutes moral behavior, but also on those of ultimate good sense; military, technological, economic and political." Like Fr. Murray, he recognizes that such arguments require for their formulation the knowledge and talents of many people representing many disciplines. Prof. O'Brien suggests the same requirement when he refers to the need for the "cooperative efforts of many empirical and normative disciplines," and Prof. Zahn recognizes it when he urges theologians to sit down with social scientists.

The inclusion of Col. Moriarty's and Prof. Dougherty's essays as the first two contributions of this symposium reflect Fr. Murray's contention that the highly complicated political and technological facts must be studied "before the moral issues involved in warfare today can be dealt with even in their generality."

The different conclusions which the contributors draw from some of the technological facts discussed in Col. Moriarty's essay illustrate the complexity of modern military strategy. There is agreement among the contributors that unlimited warfare is immoral; they would also agree that in warfare, as in every other area of human activity, means must be proportionate to ends. But what is proportionate in warfare? Where is the line to be drawn? Who is a non-combatant? How restricted must "limited war" be to remain a legitimate and moral means of defense? Will this defense still be effective? Can a nuclear war be limited? If it starts out as limited, can it remain so? On the answers to some of these questions, the contributors do not agree.

In defining the legitimate weapons of a limited war, most of the essayists refuse to exclude all nuclear weapons. Fr. Murray, Mr. Murray and Prof. O'Brien insist on the moral, rational limitation of warfare even when nuclear weapons are to be used. "To say that the possibility of limited war cannot be created by intelligence and energy, under the direction of a moral imperative," writes Fr. Murray, "is to succumb to some sort of determinism in human affairs." Prof. O'Brien reminds his readers that there are many varieties of nuclear weapons and many possible situations in which they might be used. "It would seem impossible," he says, "to encompass all these variables in one moral judgment."

While expressing general concurrence with the limited-war theorists, Col. Moriarty and Prof. Dougherty discuss the shortcomings of the doctrine from the viewpoints of military strategy and world politics. Prof. Dougherty maintains that criticisms of the limited-war idea "cannot be dismissed lightly," and says these criticisms "deserve the serious attention of those who advocate a return to the civilized tradition of limited warfare."

It is apparent from the treatment given the limited-war theory in this symposium that it will most likely remain one of the key issues in the world-wide debate over the defense policies of both East and West.

9

The reader will note that the articles by Frs. Ford and Connery are, by contrast with the other essays, rather brief. No U.S. Catholic moralist has yet written a full-scale study on nuclear war. A 48-page article, "The Morality of Obliteration Bombing," written by Fr. Ford, was published in 1944, a year before Hiroshima. The two essays selected for this symposium are not the only writings on the subject by U.S. moralists, but, in the opinion of the editor, they are two of the best. The editors of *Theology Digest* first published these (and one other article on the morality of nuclear warfare) with the comment that they "illustrate the divergence of opinion among moralists on this question." The editors went on to make an explanation that bears repeating: "When theologians disagree and the Church has not spoken, individuals who must make personal decisions (for instance, statesmen and military leaders) are thrown back on the light of their own consciences."

This may prove small consolation to the person looking for moral guidance. And it is an understandable disappointment to those people like Prof. Zahn whose own consciences are evidently not in doubt and who want Catholic spiritual leaders to declare themselves clearly against nuclear warfare. Another sociologist, C. Wright Mills, addressing himself to the clergy, says flatly: "I do not see how you can claim to be Christians and yet not speak out totally and dogmatically against the preparations and testing now under way for World War III." But many of those whose consciences *are* still in doubt are not eager to hear firm moral pronouncements that, it may be strongly suspected, would be premature and based on inadequate analyses of what the theologians term the *quaestio facti*.

A more valid complaint is not that the theologians have failed to give answers nor that the bishops have failed to make pronouncements, but that all of us — moralists, political scientists, international-law experts, sociologists, physicists, military strategists, economists, etc. — have largely failed in the task of *beginning* and encouraging the full-scale, interdisciplinary study that must be undertaken if we are to form correct consciences on war.

The Most Rev. Thomas D. Roberts, S.J., retired archbishop of Bombay who is now living in Great Britain, last summer requested the Holy See to include the moral issues of nuclear warfare in the agenda of the forthcoming ecumenical council. It is interesting to note that he suggested that preparatory work on such a study be done, not only by theologians, but by historians and economists as well.[5]

Catholic universities in the United States have an excellent opportunity to undertake a full-scale, coordinated study that would focus on the moral problems of modern war. The presence of theologians on these university faculties and the ready access to theologians of seminary faculties give them a unique advantage over other institutions of higher learning. One of the major aims of such a coordinated study would be the compilation of some of the substantive material needed for the task of forming correct consciences in this difficult area of public morality. As Fr. Murray once put it, "the instant problem is to make the traditional Christian doctrine of war relevant; and to say relevant is also to say operative, both on private thinking and on public policy." A full-scale study should utilize the best talent from many disciplines not only in Catholic universities but wherever the most competent scholars and professional people may be found. No coordinated study quite like it has ever been attempted by Cath-

[5] A fuller quotation from Archbishop Roberts' letter, sent in reply to Cardinal Tardini's circular letter to the bishops asking for council agenda suggestions, might prove of interest to the reader:

"The morality of war under modern conditions disturbs thinking people everywhere, especially in countries where freedom of conscience rules. To many who are shocked by the Church's silence on the subject, or by ambiguous pronouncements, or by lack of emphasis on the rights of conscience especially by national hierarchies, widely regarded as echoes of their respective governments, we have answers derived from our own experience as diocesan bishops obliged to compromise with conflicting national interests. But a general council should emancipate bishops, subordinating lesser loyalties to the fullness of Christian teaching in theory and practice.

"I do not suggest authoritative pronouncements which might only disturb good faith, court rebellion or disobedience, or break under the weight of vested interests where the whole national economy is now geared to war. But I do suggest setting up as preparation for the council a small body of expert theologians, historians and economists which might:

"*1*) Educate Catholic leaders in a sphere hitherto neglected; *2*) clarify issues on which guidance is sought; *3*) coordinate in a supranational atmosphere all work for peace based on fundamentals of morality.

"Incidentally this would open up common ground on which to activate the Holy Father's ideal of unity on the basis of human and religious interests common to all Religions. . . ."

olic scholarly communities. If such a study is to be truly successful, it will require a selflessness — on the part of both university and scholar — of almost heroic proportions.

Over the past few years the quality of Catholic intellectual life and the virtues and faults of Catholic higher education in the United States have been widely and openly debated. If Catholic universities meet the challenge of a coordinated study on morality and warfare, they will have done much to prove the maturity, worth and moral relevance of their academic efforts.

In conclusion let it be noted that the essays in this symposium are offered, not as final answers to the moral problems posed by modern warfare, but as guidelines and stimulants for the other studies that must follow if we are to solve the dilemma of how to stop the advance of totalitarianism without losing our own moral identity in the process.

chapter II

The Political Context

by James E. Dougherty

THE QUESTION of the morality of nuclear weapons and strategies, if it is to be discussed realistically, has to be projected against the total background of the contemporary international political environment. The judgments of the theologians, ethicians, and legalists cannot but be influenced by the granite facts and the ambiguous possibilities of the present world situation. These facts and possibilities must be weighed before we can determine whether a specific type of military strategy, or indeed any type of military strategy, can offer us some rational hope of producing effects which are ultimately good. But the task of trying to comprehend the concrete global context in which the phenomenon of modern warfare should be evaluated is appallingly complex. The epistemological difficulties involved render it almost hopeless. Notice the qualifying "almost." If the case were utterly desperate, I suppose that this paper would not have been written.

Authorities can be cited who give it as their considered opinion that the advent of nuclear military technology, plus the achievement of a certain parity in the capabilities of the Soviet Union and the United States which enable them to carry on a nip-and-tuck race, are really disguised blessings for which we should all be thankful. These developments have created, so we are told, a balance of terror (not unlike that of "two scorpions in a bottle," to use that famous and apt simile), the kind of balance which for the first time in man's history furnishes what may prove a permanent deterrent to large-scale war. Other experts, equally respected in their fields, assure us that the concept of a technological stalemate is a dangerous illusion. According to this school of thought, technology is such a dynamic and unpredictable thing as to make the notion of a permanent deterrent completely absurd. Both sides in the global struggle are portrayed as working at top speed to gain either a technological "breakthrough" or a relatively safe margin of quantitative or qualitative superiority which, if attained, may bring on an unconquerable temptation to strike a pre-emptive blow. Still other analysts proceed to bleak conclusions from premises that are in some instances pacifist, in some fatalist, and in others based upon a natural pessimism to which the study of history often leads. These contend that, even though one side does not actually achieve a breakthrough or a safety margin, general nuclear war sooner or later can be reckoned among the certainties along with death and taxes. Very frequently in trenchant terms they warn us that not the earth but the atom will have us if the psychological strains of an accelerating nuclear-missile race, with all its concomitant possibilities of miscalculation and accident, are allowed to continue for an indefinitely long period.

These rather contradictory analyses prompt one to recall a strange paradox which undoubtedly has struck many who have studied the history of international relations in the twentieth century. I refer to the various interpretations which have been put forth to explain the causes of World Wars I and II. It seems, judging from the treatment accorded the subject by many research scholars and textbook writers, that World War I broke out primarily because of the existence of an alliance system in Europe, and that World War II broke out because an effective alliance system was lacking. The inference, of course, is that if Bismarck had not started to weave the pattern of alliances in the last quarter of the nineteenth century, Europe probably would not have been plunged into war in 1914. By the same token, we are invited to conclude that if Great Britain, France, and the United States had forged a solid democratic alliance against Nazism in the mid-30s, the "unnecessary war" of 1939–1945 could have been averted.

There is no doubt that anything which has happened in history and which depended upon human decision might *not* have happened, especially if some of the circumstances had been different. But it is very unwise to manipulate the truth of human freedom in history by expounding dogmatically upon exactly what would have altered a particular course of past events or what will determine the course of future events. No one can say definitely that the alliance system caused World War I. It is quite conceivable that even *with* the alliances, war might have been avoided in 1914 through conference diplomacy. It is also conceivable that *without* a system of alliances, war would have occurred before 1920, given the conflicting nationalistic aspirations, economic rivalries, growing ideological suspicions, personality foibles and military mobilization policies which characterized the European scene after the turn of the century. Because of the complex nature of the total European background, Professor Sidney B. Fay drew this cautious conclusion concerning the alliances: Until about 1905, they helped to deter war in Europe. After that time, they contributed to the certainty that if and when war should come, it would involve all the Great Powers.

The difficulties of trying to identify the precise causes of World War II are equally formidable. Certainly the absence of a Western alliance was not the sole determining factor. The story might very well have ended differently in 1939 even without an alliance, if France and England had not furnished to the dictators such ample evidence of internal division and softness, or if a man named Hitler had never acceded to power. Conversely, it does no violence to the political imagination to speculate on the possibility that Hitler's aggressive urges and the Germans' resentment against the post-Versailles international order might have brought on war even in the face of a firm democratic alliance. The timetable perhaps would have

15

been different, but the substance of history might not have been altered. Thoughts like these can serve to make us beware of facile, mechanistic explanations of events in the political order.

The Contemporary Political Context

Now we can approach the problem of war in its contemporary political context. Since there is no such thing as "war" in the abstract — for wars are always waged between flesh-and-blood antagonists with certain national cultural characteristics, certain interests, certain ambitions, and certain irrational complexes — I shall discuss the problem in terms of the concrete relations existing between the world's premier potential belligerents: the Soviet Union and the United States. Today, men's fears of general nuclear war are largely a function of the tense confrontation of these two superpowers. Although separated geographically by thousands of miles, these two nations, thanks to modern scientific developments and communication networks, are involved in a strategic encounter that extends throughout the globe. The "front" of the Cold War is not confined to the lines which mark off the Soviet bloc from the NATO (North Atlantic Treaty Organization) countries in Europe, the Northern Tier countries in the Middle East, or the SEATO (South-East Asia Treaty Organization) countries and other American allies in Asia. It extends along the DEW (Distant Early Warning) Line in Canada. It runs through a foreign trade office of an Arab capital, a labor union congress in Havana, a university-students' organization in Tokyo. Soviet and American strategies meet at a trade fair in Jakarta, a conference of nuclear experts in Geneva, a cultural festival in Addis Ababa, or even in satellite orbits and along the pathways to the moon. Disengagement, however desirable it might be, would be no easy task.

These two powers, leaders of two huge coalitions, represent two ways of life which in their typical forms, as expressed during recent decades, present differences which are utterly unbridgeable. Both their social ideologies and their institutional structures are diametrically opposed. If it were merely a question of differing economic systems and patterns of productive-property ownership, the chances of

16

reaching an accommodation would be immeasurably better than they are. Socialist and capitalist economies can and do exist side by side and carry on friendly cooperation within the Free World. The issues that divide the world today, however, are much deeper than economic ones alone could ever be. They involve fundamental moral, political, and social values. It is unrealistic to think of the communists and the West simply as two power-blocs that are experiencing a temporary difficulty in negotiating a settlement of their misunderstandings. The bald fact is that, so long as the West insists upon remaining pluralist and free, in keeping with its own traditions, and so long as the communist bloc clings to the goals, strategy, and methods prescribed by Lenin, a meaningful settlement of differences is out of the question.

Whether we are talking about the binding character of international agreements, or elections as the basis of German unification, or colonialism, or the practical inspection system required for a workable disarmament scheme, we keep running into the unpleasant knowledge that we and the Soviets do not speak the same language. When we look out upon the world and its problems, we do not see the same thing the Soviets do. *Our* vision of the kind of universal order which we would like to see emerge is incompatible with *theirs*.

One of the most striking differences between the Western liberal society and the communist consists in the increasing willingness of the former to recognize its imperfections and discuss them openly, while the latter experiences an almost psychopathic inability to admit any deficiencies whatsoever. Communist economic plans never go awry; their rockets never misfire; they have no internal social problems; in all their international dealings they are purer than the driven snow. Perhaps the most nightmarish aspect of the new world-order which they are bent on creating is that in it there will be no room for mistakes — at least not by the party rulers. Individuals, of course, will always be given an opportunity to express their carefully rehearsed *mea culpa*'s in open court, but no one will be allowed to criticize the omniscient leadership for such decisions (concerning other Hungarys and other Tibets) as may be deemed necessary from time to time to consolidate the people's revolution. Although it is

17

hard for a Christian to admit, it does seem at times that we do not belong to the same world — we and the Leninists. Yet we must share it with them. Perhaps at some deep, mysterious level, discernible only to God, the presence of the Leninists on this planet is good for us. Certainly we are under an obligation to love our enemies, and the Leninists have spared no effort to put us to the test on that score. But our human reason, which grace perfects rather than destroys, tells us that we must resist the spread of communism; for if that system triumphs, or rather where it triumphs, Christian or any other spiritual tradition as such is erased, and a new, purely materialistic interpretation of the meaning of life on earth is substituted. Christians should occasionally remind themselves of this brutal fact before passing adverse judgment on the defense policies of Western nations. Western governments may deserve criticism for the form in which they have cast their defense policies, but not for their preoccupation with the problem itself.

Massive Retaliation

Unfortunately, the West's experience of two total wars in the twentieth century has left a deep imprint on the thinking of its peoples, strategists, and statesmen. The West was confronted in the post-World War II situation by an aggressive communist bloc commanding superior resources in terms of conventional armies, guerrilla forces, and a paramilitary international subversive apparatus. The problem seemed particularly acute at the end of the Korean War, the most frustrating conflict ever engaged in by the American people, who were not at all accustomed to a war begun over a principle of justice ending in a stalemate. With guerrilla wars still in progress in Malaya and Indochina, the Western alliance feared that it might be maneuvered into fighting a series of engagements around the periphery of the Sino-Soviet bloc on terms favorable to the communists. As a stopgap to the threat of creeping communist expansion, the United States committed itself to the avowed policy of "massive retaliation." This policy, announced by U.S. Secretary of State John Foster Dulles, introduced an element of doubt about the future response of the United States to acts of communist aggression.

18

By adopting the policy of massive retaliation, the United States hoped to frighten the Soviets out of their peripheral arson.

It was generally assumed that the policy of massive retaliation meant that the United States would reply to an attack, not only on the NATO area but on the "grey areas" as well, with nuclear strikes by the SAC (Strategic Air Command) against the Soviet Union and communist China. Those who took it for granted that the policy looked to the annihilation of the major population-industrial centers of the communist bloc roundly condemned it as immoral and uncivilized. Others, proceeding from strategic premises, condemned the doctrine of massive retaliation as incredible. The communist leaders, they insisted, would not allow themselves to be deterred by such an unbelievable threat, since America would never risk all-out nuclear war over a piece of territory in Asia which the vast majority of Americans would have a hard time locating on a map.

The communist leaders may not have taken the doctrine of massive retaliation to mean exactly what its American critics took it to mean. Even though they may have felt certain that the United States would not start a global nuclear war over a remote border violation, perhaps they feared that atomic weapons would be employed against communist military targets, either at the point of conflict or elsewhere. In 1954 that might have meant either a local communist defeat or else a very reluctant communist decision to opt for general war (for which they were ill-prepared at the time). Secretary Dulles did not say when, where, with what kind of weapons, or against what type of targets the United States would retaliate. The very vagueness of the policy may have served a useful purpose by furnishing a psychological deterrent to further communist conventional-weapon attacks. The fact remains that, since the policy was announced, Sino-Soviet strategists have launched no new "brush-fire" wars. American policy makers do not deserve to be blamed too much for thinking that the avowed policy of massive retaliation has had some measure of success since 1954. We cannot categorically deny that such a policy may have contributed something toward shifting the conflict between the communist bloc and the West from the realm of direct military engagement to the more subtle realms of economic, political,

19

and psychological warfare. This, however, is not at all to suggest that the policy of massive retaliation is necessarily of enduring effectiveness. Perhaps it is no more than a function of a particular phase in the military-technological race between the Soviet Union and the United States. Nevertheless, governmental institutions have a peculiar way of turning relatively temporary pragmatic successes into permanent cornerstones of national policy. If a certain type of policy seems to work for a few years, it tends to take on the character of unquestionability within the ranks of officialdom.

Limited War

One of the results flowing from American experience in the Korean War and from the enunciation of the highly controversial massive-retaliation doctrine has been a debate among Western strategists over the possibility of limited war. A number of writers [1] have attempted to set forth the feasibility of employing atomic weapons in a limited and discriminating manner to deter, repel, or defeat less-than-total communist aggression. This school has contended that, unless the Soviets can be persuaded that Western strategists are refining their concepts of nuclear warfare to make room for limited nuclear warfare, there is a grave danger that the massive-retaliation doctrine will be increasingly regarded as American bluff, as the Soviets develop their nuclear-missile capabilities to the point where they can deter the deterrent. Furthermore, argue those strategists who seek a doctrine of limited encounter, if we continue to take it for granted that when military conflict finally comes it will inevitably assume the shape of global push-button war, then we shall be under intolerable pressure to execute immediately an all-out strategic plan once the crisis is reached, even though it means mutual suicide. Therefore, they have made an effort to devise a strategic theoretical framework in which a number of distinctions can be drawn; especially distinctions between types of nuclear weapons to be employed

[1] Among those who have advocated limited-war strategy have been Henry A. Kissinger, Sir Anthony Buzzard, Sir John Slessor, Arnold Wolfers, Robert Osgood, Denis Healey, Raymond Aron, Bernard Brodie, Thomas E. Murray, Paul A. Nitze, Colonel Richard Leghorn, General James M. Gavin, and A. T. Hadley.

(i.e., atomic and thermonuclear weapons) and between the kind of targets against which they would be used (strictly military installations rather than civilian population centers).

Against the concept of limited war in the nuclear age, if taken to mean a direct military encounter between Soviet and American forces, a number of objections have been raised. These objections, when examined altogether, are by no means entirely consistent with each other, nor are they unanswerable on strategic grounds, but the fact remains that they have been prevalent in circles where policy is formed.

1. Certain geographic areas of the world (especially Western Europe) are so strategically sensitive and so important that it is practically impossible to imagine a war there remaining "limited."

2. The Europeans themselves are frightened by talk of a limited-war strategy for NATO, because they interpret it to mean that, if war should come over an issue such as Berlin, it would be fought out almost exclusively on European soil. Many Europeans would feel safer if both the Soviets and the Americans took it for granted that should war break out it will be carried immediately to each other's home territory. Such an anticipation, they think, will help to make Washington and Moscow much more cautious in their handling of "in-between" disputes.

3. In an age of intense ideological Cold War, it is highly probable that no conflict in which Soviet and American forces were ranged against each other could really be fought for limited objectives and kept limited in the manner of its waging. The powerful exigencies of communist and Western prestige would very likely prevent either side from accepting any result that might appear as a limited defeat.

4. The ruthless dialectic of modern military technology works against the feasibility of a limited war between powers possessing nuclear capabilities. For years Soviet propaganda has been directed to the task of convincing us and the world that the notion of limited atomic war is absurd. Perhaps the Soviets have succeeded in persuading both themselves and many in the West. Perhaps if another case of easily identifiable communist military aggression occurs, and atomic weapons are introduced by either side, our national excitatory

21

processes will be overstimulated and we shall, almost unwittingly, deliver a cataclysmic blow. In a period of profound psychological crisis, the American people may be sorely tempted "to take up arms against a sea of troubles and, by opposing, end them."

5. For this last reason, there is also a grave risk in equipping either American or Allied ground forces with nuclear weapons. In the event of a local, accidental skirmish, field commanders posted in advanced European positions might feel under pressure to respond to attack with all the firepower at their disposal. Hence not a few military men and statesmen in the West have recently gone so far as to urge the development of an adequate level of conventional, nonatomic forces to cope with the potential range of intermediate communist attack.

These criticisms of the limited-war idea cannot be dismissed lightly and they deserve the serious attention of those who advocate a return to the "civilized" tradition of limited warfare. But the most ardent advocates, and similarly the severest critics, of the limited-war strategy often fail to come to grips with the full reality of the present global situation. Most of them are inclined to analyze the problem of limited war in a historical vacuum. Conditioned by the experience of the Korean War, they want to prepare the United States for a repetition of that type of communist-Western conflict. They do not always seem to realize that the Western and the communist approaches to conflict are fundamentally divergent, and that the concept of limited war (especially as it has developed since Korea) does not mean the same thing to Western and communist strategists.

The idea of keeping war limited for moral and humanitarian reasons, and of using no greater force in war than is necessary to accomplish a rational political objective, is deep-rooted in Western culture. The revival of this notion in the nuclear age represents a commendable effort to resolve the dichotomy of modern Western strategic thought, polarized as it is between the extremes of absolute pacifism and the militarism of total war. Both the pacifists and the militarists have managed with equal effectiveness to drive a wedge between military strategy and ethics, the former by contending that the employment of force to defend the moral order is never justified, and

22

the latter by refusing to place any moral boundaries on the use of force. The advocates of limited war are sincerely trying to end the schism which rends the modern Western mind and which has led in this century to a tragic alternation between increasingly grotesque wars of mass slaughter and increasingly grandiose schemes for perpetual peace. The Western mind today is scarcely capable of discerning on the strategic horizon any other alternatives than all-out nuclear mutual annihilation or a policy of peace-at-any-price. The strategy of limited war furnishes a solution to this dilemma. Properly developed, it could be the best solution.

Protracted Conflict

The concept of limited war as usually set forth, however, leaves something to be desired; for although it meets the requirements of moral action as understood in the light of the Western, Christian, traditional doctrine of war, it does not seem to be well suited to the contemporary strategic situation. As a concept, it is a product of Western culture. There is nothing in communist doctrine which corresponds exactly to it. In planning and conducting international conflict, the communist strategist does not knowingly submit to any limitations of a spiritual, ethical, or humane character. The only limitations which he recognizes are those which are imposed by the laws of physics, geography, politics, economics, and psychology. Within these limits, he strives to integrate all available modes of conflict into a multidimensional scheme. His goal is a total one — nothing less than universal hegemony following the annihilation of the Western world as a viable system. But his understanding of "annihilation," too, may be radically different from ours.

In Western usage, a strategy of annihilation necessarily implies a total war in which a maximal amount of physically destructive power is brought to bear upon the enemy to force his unconditional surrender or his obliteration within the shortest possible time. When we think of annihilation, we always think at the same time of a frontal strategy and a decisive military encounter. Even in our discussions of limited war, we cannot escape our "frontalist" philosophy. We look to specific, easily identifiable military challenges in specific geo-

23

graphic areas. We envision fully-equipped armies smashing across a national boundary and thereby committing an old-fashioned act of aggression. This, however, is the very kind of challenge which the communist strategist of protracted conflict is most loathe to hurl down before us, especially while we are prepared for it.

The global conflict, as the communists view it, is one of indefinite duration. They possess what we might call strategic patience, a quality which is in rather short supply among Americans. Strategic patience demands an appreciation of the meaning of time as a strategic fourth dimension. Whereas our cultural tradition and our psychological structure both incline us to yearn for the decisive encounter (whether total or limited), the communist aim is to keep the conflict with the West indecisive at any one time or place so long as there remains any doubt how an all-out battle would turn out. They will in all probability forego the frontal assault until the world-power balance has shifted overwhelmingly in their favor, if it ever does. They are, we must remember, firmly convinced that time is on their side. With each passing decade, their over-all strategic position, measured in terms of economico-technological growth and political prestige, shows improvement. To the extent that the communist high command maintains contact with the order of rationality, it is unlikely that it will risk an Armagedon for the sake of marginal territorial gain. There is no reason to suppose that the Soviet leaders trust Western statements concerning the feasibility of limited war in the nuclear age. They cannot be sure that, once atomic weapons are introduced into an engagement, traditional concepts of civilized warfare will prevail. Hence they are extremely cautious about gambling on peripheral aggression.

But this does not mean that the current international situation is a stalemate. Like every form of dynamic totalitarianism, the communist system is bent on power accumulation at the expense of other states. Against the military defenses thrown up by the Western nations to contain them, communists have continued to advance by employing a weapons-spectrum that is not confined to military hardware but encompasses all possible relationships — political, economic, psychological, cultural, and technological — between states and social groups. Its arsenal includes propaganda, trade agreements, disarmament negotiations, cultural-exchange programs, sociological "wedge-driving," and educational activities. The indirect approach to conflict at which the communists excel seems particularly suited to an international environment which furnishes endless opportunities for promoting mischief. The communists have been able to carry out their assault against the West through a variety of proxies and auxiliaries: satellite governments; conspiratorial parties; partitioned states; neutralist, nationalist, pacifist, and anticolonialist movements; guerrilla armies; and all manner of "front" organizations. Their strategy, which is characterized by a constant shifting of operational tactics, apparently prescribes the gradual defeat of the West over a relatively long period by piecemeal conquests, feints, maneuvers, diplomatic turnabouts, economic experiments and forays, social penetrations, psychological manipulations, and various forms of violence — all of which fall below the threshold of provoking the West into unleashing its atomic weapons.

Rarely in history have men been treated to the spectacle of such a skillfully executed plan of psychologico-social warfare as that developed by Lenin, Stalin, Khrushchev and Mao. The target of the campaign is Western society as a whole: its elite groups with all their unique, liberal ideals; its institutional structure; its popular aspirations and emotions; and its opinion-molding and decision-making machinery. Several methods are used, but most of them can be reduced to the Pavlovian process of conditioning, projected on an international scale. Irritating tensions are built up for a while and then relaxed. Balm is soothingly rubbed over a sore spot on the organism while pin-prick stimuli are applied elsewhere. Ambiguous themes are played on the propaganda apparatus, like the ringing of high and low frequency bells. Threats of apocalyptic thermonuclear destruction are alternated with the blandishments of peaceful coexistence; the interval between them is reduced until they become almost indistinguishable and the target social organism approaches the point of psychological disturbance. The international conditioning process, carried on largely through the West's own mass media, is also employed in a weird Freudian reverse to induce neurotic guilt complexes, fears, frustrations, doubts, and loss of self-confidence within the West. All of these in turn, so it is hoped, will lead to confusion of purpose, corrosion of political will, and policy paralysis within the Atlantic nations.

In the meantime, the communists confidently expect that their economic system, whose productive levels are not yet quite half those of the West, will expand at a more rapid rate than the latter and gradually overtake it. As the "socialist world market" grows through economic penetration, Western countries will find their foreign markets contracting and hence will be tempted to engage increasingly in internecine economic warfare. They are sure, too, that technological prowess will develop faster under conditions created by the centralized allocation of all industrial resources than under the conditions which prevail in a free-market economy. Communist organizational proficiency will improve, while Western governmental agencies dissipate their energies, in a sort of riot of official pluralism, wrangling over the proper defense and foreign policies to be pursued. The Western alliance as time goes on will be more and more beset by insoluble political dilemmas and internal economic contradictions. This will be particularly true in the erstwhile colonial areas, where the West's historic influence will continue to disintegrate steadily and where nascent states must inevitably incline toward socialist solutions of their pressing development problems. Communism, so its adherents believe, has passed the critical period in which its future hung in doubt. It is now riding the tide of history. Ultimate success is assured, so long as foolish adventuresomeness and risky gambling are avoided.

We may, if we wish, dismiss the foregoing convictions as a lot of Marxist-Leninist-Stalinist-Khrushchevist-Maoist buncombe. But there is an impressive amount of evidence attesting to the fact that the communists take these notions seriously and use them as guidelines in the formulation of policy. Whether their interpretation of history conforms to the evolving international reality or not, it merits an effort on our part to understand it as an important factor in the contemporary strategic situation. If we fail to understand it, we shall undoubtedly go on attributing to the communists theories of war which are peculiarly Western in shape and are not geared to the Soviet outlook. Certainly we should put out of our minds the image of a Soviet leadership that is just waiting for the West to furnish a *casus belli*. The Soviets may issue profuse threats of general nuclear-missile warfare in times of international crisis in order to hold the Western nations at bay, and to keep them from intervening in a peripheral trouble spot and restoring a noncommunist order of stability. But up to the present time, Soviet threats have not been a reliable guide to genuine Soviet intentions. The aftermath of the American landings in Lebanon, close to the borders of the Soviet Union, constituted an ample demonstration of that fact. The Soviets were undoubtedly embarrassed by the Western intervention in the Middle East during the summer of 1958, but their deftness in putting the best face on an awkward situation reflected a rather high degree of strategic sophistication.

Four Basic Facts

When we talk about deterrence, nuclear stalemate, and limited war, we ought to remind ourselves of four very basic facts. 1. The first fifteen years of the nuclear age have been marked by frequent international wars or civil wars and sporadic uprisings with international implications.[2] 2. In almost all of these violent conflicts, the communists have played one role or another, either by furnishing military or guerrilla forces, "volunteers," arms, advice, or political, diplomatic, and propaganda support. 3. In none of them, however, has the Soviet Union formally committed its forces into action against the United States or against any country with which the United States has a binding treaty of defense. 4. Further, none of these conflicts have been of a type in which the introduction of nuclear weapons would have made much sense. Either military or political common sense has worked against their use.

This is a picture of what the international situation has been since the end of World War II. But the technological background has been

[2] The scenes of conflict have included: China, Malaya, the Philippines, Indochina, Greece, Kashmir, the Arab-Israeli sector (twice), Korea, Guatemala, Algeria, Cyprus, Egypt, Hungary, Oman, Indonesia (twice), Lebanon-Jordan, Iraq, the Formosa Straits, Cuba, Tibet, and Laos.

27

changing, as Col. Moriarty points out trenchantly in the paper that follows. The undisputed nuclear superiority which the United States held in the age of the long-range bomber is now in the process of being considerably diminished as we move into the age of intercontinental missiles. I do not mean to suggest that the Soviets have already gained a decisive margin over the West in the missile field. I personally do not think that they have and most certainly hope that they do not. The international strategic situation will become much more dangerously unstable than it has been in the last decade if they do gain such a margin, or, worse still, if they think they have gained such a margin when in fact they have not. From here on, the very life of mankind may hinge upon the accuracy of intelligence estimates more than it is comfortable to contemplate. Epistemological problems and psychological strains may overwhelm rational strategic thinking and give both sides nervous "trigger fingers."

If Soviet strategy does follow the pattern of protracted conflict, whence arises the danger? Several extremely dangerous possibilities lie ahead. As Soviet missile power grows, the communists, thinking that they have successfully neutralized the West's deterrent power, may grow emboldened to embark upon local aggression in a peripheral area, such as Formosa or one of the small, weak countries of Southeast Asia. Communist strategists might deem it safer to make the "grab" attempt with non-Soviet, nonatomic forces (probably Chinese units) which would be quantitatively unmatchable in respect to the time required to bring an adequate counterforce to bear upon the situation. Or, the Soviets themselves might create a crisis in Europe by making a strategic though nonviolent move; e.g., unilaterally altering the status of West Berlin vis-à-vis East Germany (as they have frequently threatened to do). The day might come when moves such as these will be looked upon essentially as shrewd psychological gambits rather than actual military operations. The Soviets might think that in the face of such moves, especially if accompanied by dire threats of rocket warfare, the United States will be frightened into inaction and into an acceptance of the *fait accompli.* If the Soviet calculation proves correct, it will mean that the international legal order can be violated with impunity. The West would lose an extremely critical round in the psycho-political struggle, and the Western alliance would probably start to disintegrate. But on the other hand, the Soviets are not infallible and they may miscalculate the American-Western response. Rather than become subject to a whole series of similar blackmail actions, the West may decide that it must deliver a riposte. The question then will be what kind of operation should be undertaken. At the present time, we seem incapable of thinking about anything except massive retaliation.

As an operational doctrine, massive retaliation, taken in its usual meaning, never made sense. As an avowed policy, it may have served a useful purpose and it may, for all we know, still be serving a useful purpose. This, no doubt, must sound like perfect casuistry. But the present world situation has just about reached the point of complete ambiguity. I for one would hesitate to say with certainty that we should, at this time, publicly renounce the concept of thermonuclear deterrence. I am not sure what an upsetting, possibly even calamitous, effect it might have upon the precarious international balance. If the fear of mutual incineration is slowly improving the practical wisdom and self-restraint of the Soviets and ourselves, and making us at least think seriously about the problems and methods of phased arms control; then it may be very imprudent for us to change our course too quickly. By rejecting a strategy based on the notion of thermonuclear strikes, we may earn some short-term political benefits. We may also think quite sincerely that such a repudiation is morally necessary, because this public policy and its weapons-establishment could lead to history's greatest moral disaster.

But at the same time, we may unwittingly create a situation in which communist military aggression against a weaker country will again seem profitable, before we have had a chance to build up an adequate, substitute defense. The cause of morality is not very well served by shifting from a situation in which war is deterred to one in which it is not. Since World War II, we have been preoccupied with a deterrent capability which perhaps does serve a useful and moral purpose so long as it actually deters, but which would probably become immoral in the manner of its use if it failed as a deterrent. The heart of the moral-strategic problem confronting us, it seems, is

29

this: How can we change over from our existing deterrent capability to a different type of deterrent capability which would prove equally, or even more, effective in holding aggressors at bay; and which, if it ever became necessary, could be made operational in a moral way? The nature of the fast-changing technological order itself, combined with the fact that American leadership is beginning to cast around for a more satisfactory strategy, offers certain possibilities which will bear exploration. There are grounds for hoping that over the course of the next five years or so, if we really bend our efforts to the task, we may be able to escape from our moral dilemma and devise a more rational strategic policy. I suggest that we could do this while completing the transition from the prerocket to the rocket age.

Toward a More Moral Strategy

With weapons systems undergoing constant refinement, we ought to be able, at the same time, to refine them in the moral dimension. It may take several years to make meaningful progress in this direction, but fortunately the world strategic situation is such that we may be granted the necessary time for the transformation. We are engaged in a protracted struggle, and we must strive to think in long-range terms, even in our moral analysis of the problem. Individuals may experience moral conversion within a relatively short time span; but nations can hardly be expected to undergo profound changes of thought overnight, and this is precisely what most pacifists demand that they do. The concepts which guide governmental institutions are modified only very gradually and with painstaking effort. All that I am suggesting is that, although persons and states are subjected to the same fundamental code of justice and the same norms of the natural law, they are not subjected to them in exactly the same mode. If individuals sometimes need a little time to extricate themselves from moral dilemmas, states need more. The doctrinaire moralist can thunder at governments from now until doomsday, blasting their policies as irrational and immoral, and insisting that they be altered immediately. In all likelihood, he will accomplish nothing because established (as distinct from revolutionary) governments seldom adopt radical solutions to any problem. If there is validity in the Aristotelian-Thomistic-Burkean principle that whatever genuine progress is made in the political order is made as a result of slow constructive growth and gradual reform, then the lesson ought to be applicable in this sphere, too. We have been imperceptibly drifting into our present moral-strategic dilemma for years, and it may take several more years to disengage ourselves from its horns.

It is incumbent upon morally-concerned citizens to ponder carefully the complexities and the subtleties of the strategic problems confronting the Free World. The unending debate over national defense policy must be brought back onto the track of rationality. In order to do this, we must avoid simplist solutions. We should be sufficiently competent to advance our arguments not only on the grounds of what constitutes moral behavior, but also on those of ultimate good sense, military, technological, economic, and political. We need strategic minds to discern the shifting realities of the international environment and the dynamics of power relations; we need scientific minds to advise us on the manifold possibilities of weapons technology so that we can make the best choices for allocation of our national resources; we need economic minds which can penetrate into the mysteries of industrial growth rates, defense budgeting and governmental fiscal policies; we need sociologists and psychologists who have studied the phenomena of tensions, fears, and animosities which mar the relations of ideologically divergent societies; we need political analysts who understand the realities of the systemic revolution through which the world is passing, the role of governments and diplomacy in this revolution, the temper of world opinion, the connection between armament contests and disarmament negotiations, and the possibilities of accommodation between our own open, liberal society and the closed, totalitarian society of the Sino-Soviet bloc. Above all, we need ethical and theological knowledge, spiritual formation, and the aid of grace to be able to discern good and evil tendencies of policy, to promote the former and discourage the latter. These we need desperately if we would

31

dare enter into the complex process of helping to shape history in the nuclear age — through criticism, suggestion, persuasion, advice, and otherwise influencing the minds of men on issues so crucial.

The initial objective of our efforts should be some perceptible movement toward a more moral strategy. Who can say but that every small impulse in this direction may serve to gain us more time and more wisdom? While working toward a rationalization of our defense establishment as a sure goal, without arbitrary deadlines, we may suddenly find ourselves able to take modest yet worthwhile experimental steps toward a practical and fully enforceable arms control scheme whose successive phases would prove consonant with a legitimate desire for security, instead of being conducive only to gnawing uncertainty. With each month gained, the international scene changes and new opportunities to stabilize the world order and satisfy the aspirations of peoples appear on the horizon. Western Europe is re-emerging as an important region of creative vitality, economically and politically. The old imperial powers have either given up their positions of overseas dominance or else they are trying to found new associations upon voluntary consent and mutual advantage, rather than force and exploitation. Dozens of new states, still weak and poor, are proudly asserting their determination to maintain their independence and to develop their economies. Each year, new channels of international cooperation and economic assistance are opened between the West and the underdeveloped countries. The pace has been slow, but now is quickening, and results are becoming noticeable. West Germany and Japan have recovered their positions of strength in the international community and are now playing a constructive role in world affairs. Meanwhile, inside the Soviet Union there are some signs that communism as an ideology and as an organization may be undergoing a change for the better under the impact of cultural-exchange programs, tourism, and internal social and technological developments. Whether communism as a doctrine and method of international power conflict is also being modified remains to be seen. The much-vaunted policy shifts of recent years may be either feigned or real. The West has been fooled enough times in the past by the apparently beneficent transformations of the Soviet system to know better than to expect too much. We must not forget that Lenin once restored the capitalists in Russia, and Stalin once granted the world's most liberal-looking constitution. Every spring thaw is followed sooner or later by another Siberian winter. It may take a decade or more before we can properly judge whether international tensions have relaxed to the point where arms control with security can be achieved.

If we lift our eyes from the purely military battlefield, which is now ominously quiet, and gaze at the broader international background in all its variety, we can find some justification for allowing our hopes to stir faintly. If we set ourselves to the task which we all feel incumbent upon us — the task of trying to lift the national debate up to a moral level in terms which men of good will can understand — perhaps we can yet help to turn mankind back from the precipice. There may very well be enough time to complete the task, but precious little time left to begin it.

chapter III

Technology, Strategy and National Military Policy

by John K. Moriarty

Early in 1958 Neil H. McElroy, then secretary of defense, made the following statement in defense appropriations hearings before a committee of the House of Representatives:

It seems to me, and there appears to be general agreement on this point, that we are moving rapidly into a period of increasing danger — not only to ourselves but also to the U.S.S.R. and indeed to the people of all the world. This situation is not the result of anything we, alone, have done or failed to do. It is the inevitable consequence of the explosive progress in science and technology which is making available a succession of weapons of ever-increasing destructiveness and speed of delivery.

One can sympathize with a worried soap manufacturer, temporarily burdened with responsibility for his nation's military forces, in this assessment of the international situation. One can also commend him. For embodied in his remark was more honesty, if not more confidence and hope, than most political commentary today allows itself — whether it is defending or attacking national military policy.

Indeed, the present military confrontation in the world is perilous.

It will, of course, be said that any war must be perilous, and that the difference is only one of degree. A difference in degree can amount to a difference in kind. If a total war is fought in the next few years it will be a different kind of war from the total wars of the past. Elementary computations of known capabilities indicate that an all-out nuclear war would leave scores of millions of noncombatants dead and would wreck much of civilization in its present form. In the words of Secretary McElroy: "There appears to be general agreement on this point."

Secretary McElroy is also correct in indicating that this state of affairs has been made possible by advances in technology. He is wrong, however, in his implication that we ourselves have no responsibility in the matter. Technology has indeed constructed a remarkable and constantly expanding edifice. It is almost as if an automatic computer, having been set to work on a problem, began to use its own completed calculations in order to reason to others beyond the intentions or capabilities of its initiator. But here, in truth, man's lack of control is only a question of degree. For centuries there have been continuing technological changes carrying with them potentially catastrophic consequences to some men if other men were allowed to have their uninhibited way — developments in science, in agriculture, in manufacturing, in transportation, in war-making. But men have also devised practical political means, both formal and informal, to bring these innovations more or less under control, so that their use or misuse would not be irrevocably subject to the whims of a few men completely insulated from the will of their fellows. The technology of war seems, however, to have become a huge, unwieldy monster, unhindered by the kinds of political controls which in the past have acted as brakes upon earlier technological hazards. Men have aided and abetted this military-technological breakaway, instead of attempting to control it. They cannot, then, blame "technology." The basis for political control over technology is present in the United States today. Before this control can be asserted, however, there is required a most careful analysis of the problem being faced. An introduction to such an analysis will be essayed in this article.

Far too much time has elapsed already. To appreciate this fact,

35

one has only to look at the terms in which the problem is currently stated: survival, balance of terror, massive retaliation, continuous alert, preventive war, pre-emptive war ("We won't strike first unless you do"), circle of complete destruction, etc. Modern military-political concepts apparently can be expressed only in superlatives, extremes and absolutes. Yet the process by which war took this form passed almost unnoticed. We woke one morning and found ourselves prisoners of the changed concept and the changed technology. As Arnold Toynbee remarked: "Like other evils, war has an insidious way of appearing not intolerable until it has secured such a stranglehold upon the lives of its addicts that they no longer have the power to escape from its grip when its deadliness has become manifest." Men, of course, can escape. But they will not do so by either entering into a state of shock and calling frantically for immediate (and unenforceable) disarmament and world federation, or by flogging the technological genie to produce ever more advanced and terrible weapons at a faster and faster rate. Escape from thralldom will come through a recognition that going to war should be the result of a policy choice, not an accident, and that the weapons, tactics, and strategy of warfare should similarly be decided upon through institutionalized processes which at the very least give access to nonmilitary dissenters who support broader values. Such processes do not adequately exist in the United States today. And yet, if the argument of this paper — and this book — is correct, the national security, the moral integrity, and even the existence of the United States as a social organism may depend on its ability to solve the problem of modern war.

The Changing Nature of Military Technology

There was a time when nations contemplating war were reasonably certain of the weapons with which the war was going to be fought. Technology produced improvements in weapons only sporadically, and incorporation of the improvements into tactics and strategy was usually slow. Today the technological process of research-and-development for new weapons is not only rapid, it is continuous, and accelerating. New weapons often cannot be gotten into production because continual changes keep their final engineering specifications unwritten. Weapons already in production, such as the Air Force B-47 medium-range jet bomber, have been delayed in reaching the operational units because they were sent back into modification plants as soon as they came off the production line. Others, like the B-36 long-range bomber, were often unavailable operationally for long periods because they were continually being recycled through major modification stages; the B-36 went through six such cycles, during which a three and one-half million dollar airplane gradually became a six and one-half million dollar airplane. This unending process of technological improvement has, by imperceptible stages, taken on the nature of an objective in itself. The latest weapon is always being rushed into production and on to the operational units; it is hardly in their hands, however, before its successor appears in sight following the same course. War becomes wholly dependent upon technology. The opponent, meanwhile, loses the character of flesh and blood, and becomes, in effect, a set of performance specifications which one's latest weapon-system does not quite meet.

Whoever controls this technological process controls the nature of modern war. Yet the strange fact is that the military services, at least in the United States, can only with the gravest of qualifications be said to be in control of military technology. In the first place, they do not develop and produce their own weapons. "Industry" does this for them; under military guidance and direction, of course. But "military guidance" often consists of following in a direction already determined by the scientists and industrialists, or of maintaining administrative supervision over various projects by means of either liaison officers (who may be civilians) or progress reports and over-all budgetary controls. This military dependence on science and industry is, if anything increasing. Nonmilitary consultants are even making major contributions to the military's administrative and operational processes; witness, for example, the relationship of the RAND Corporation to the Air Force.

To understand fully the extent to which weapons development and planning are separated from actual military operations, it must be

37

recognized that the split between these functions *within* military services is just as marked. When the military presents its budget to Congress, for example, many of the witnesses have only a very general understanding of the specific items they are defending. Random questions by congressmen (they can only be random questions) are, as likely as not, answered on the following day after high priority telephone calls or wires from the Pentagon to the experts. This is not improper. Today's age is one of specialization; we probably could not operate in any other way. Indeed, the military already wastes too much time and money trying to have available detailed information to answer possible questions from higher administrative levels or from Congress. But the fact still remains that there is a considerable gulf between the weapon-developers and the weapon-users. Because of this gulf there is not either in the executive or legislative branch really effective control of weapons development, of weapons use, of military tactics, and of military strategy.

In the process described above the gradual transformation of the objective of war has been speeded. From "military victory" this objective gradually became the "destruction of the enemy," with the "enemy" being not only soldiers but an entire society. This did not happen because the technicians were more bloodthirsty than the military. It happened because they were technicians and pursued their technical objectives. The American military leaders, because of their distance from actual operations and because they were a part of the social system which interpreted war as a struggle to destroy inhuman evildoers, concurred in the transformation. But the military leaders and the political leaders have no answer to the final indictment: We find ourselves today with a predominant military technology, tactics, and strategy which cannot "win" wars in any moral or just sense, and cannot win them in some practical senses.

This situation came about because the technicians took what they understood to be the primary means of warfare and set about improving them. For many years it has been the custom to speak of requirements for military weapons primarily in terms of "destructiveness" and "speed of delivery," or of "firepower" and "mobility." Gustavus Adolphus' dragoons, the eighteenth century's precision maneuvers, "gallant Pelham's" charges with artillery, the mating of the airplane and the nuclear bomb have all been efforts to improve the mobility of concentrated firepower. For a true picture of modern war, of course, one must keep in mind the long and intricate military-industrial process involved in bringing a weapon's firepower to effective use; research, development, testing, production, personnel training, maintenance, target selection, "prestrike" reconnaissance; to mention only a few of the more obvious elements. But the basic objective has always been delivery of destructive power. In recent decades this destructive power has increasingly been sought in terms of its purely *explosive* potential.

The development of the atomic bomb was obviously a major breakthrough in the progress of this quest. Comparisons of the explosive power of a thermonuclear bomb in terms of its equivalent in the TNT dropped by all the bombers in World War II have become commonplace. Sometimes, however, in this mass obeisance paid to the power of nuclear weapons, two related but divergent facts have been ignored: First, the great thermonuclear weapons in the megaton range (a megaton corresponding to the energy equivalent of one *million* tons of TNT) should not even be compared with the low-kiloton (one kiloton equaling a *thousand* tons of TNT) range weapons in such matters as area of destruction and radioactive fallout; second, the effects of the kiloton-range weapons, even in the smallest "tactical" sizes, cannot be compared with the TNT weapons of World War II.[1]

Delivery systems have made almost comparable progress. As the Washington Center of Foreign Policy Research pointed out in its December, 1959, study for the Committee on Foreign Relations of the United States Senate: "The accelerating rate of progress in military technology is illustrated by the fact that manned aircraft did

---

[1] The general public is well aware of the effects of a multimegaton weapon if exploded in a surface-burst upon a large city. For example, the Joint Committee on Atomic Energy in its hearings on "The Biological and Environmental Effects of Nuclear War," June 22–26, 1959, assumed a mock attack wherein six million people died in New York City alone, from two 10-megaton weapons. But even "tactical" nuclear weapons of 1-kiloton size would cause the complete destruction of frame houses and similar structures within a circle one-half mile in diameter.

not succeed in breaking the sound "barrier" in level flight until 1947, but attained speeds twice that of sound in 1953 and triple that of sound 3 years later."

Missiles have progressed even faster than manned aircraft. Whereas in 1945 the Germans were shooting V-2 rockets at London a little over 200 miles away with only occasional accuracy, today both the Soviet Union and the United States are claiming for their ICBMs (Inter-Continental Ballistic Missiles) distances of 6,000 to 8,000 miles or even greater, with degrees of accuracy ranging from 1 to 2 miles. Whether these claims are completely reliable or not is beside the point. They are not at all implausible today, however, and they will certainly be surpassed by actual capabilities in the next few years. Comparable progress will be made in antimissile missiles, reconnaissance satellites, satellite systems for world-wide communication and navigation, and even space vehicles. Missiles at the present time are undoubtedly in the same relative stage of development as aircraft were in World War I.

The present military predilection for rapid, long-range delivery of massive destructive power dominates the art of war. It has thus created an international military-technological situation with several dominant characteristics. One of these is that the present arms race is practically closed to all but the two superpowers. The immense resources required to develop and produce complete operational weapon-systems are simply not available to lesser nations. A limited capability in certain weapons is of course possible to such countries as Great Britain, France, communist China, and several others. But such a capability could never induce a "rational decision" on the part of one of these countries to go to war if an eventual opponent might be one of the two great powers. Without other complementary offensive and defensive elements, a limited weapons capability would merely be an invitation to national destruction if the system's purely blackmailing, deterrent threat failed.

A second characteristic of the present international situation is its rigidity. In spite of rapid and continuous technological changes, the very complexity of modern weapons is such that "lead time" (the time that must elapse between the statement of a weapon's original design characteristics and actual delivery of the completed weapon to its intended users) becomes an increasingly important factor. The missiles the United States is flying today were on the drawing board before 1950. Thus, a nation cannot decide in one year that it wishes to take a completely fresh approach to a particular threat possibly arising three or four years from now.[2] The United States, for example, is already committed for the next eight or ten years in regard to its more complex weapon-systems. Any reduction of lead times will, of course, increase a nation's area of choice and flexibility in meeting future threats. A relevant facet of this problem is the report that Soviet lead times are consistently about half the length of those of the United States. This may possibly indicate a difference in basic capabilities of the respective technological systems. On the other hand it may, and very likely does, represent a difference in clearness of objective and willingness to make special efforts to reach the objective.

A third characteristic of the present military-technological situation is that it tends to produce and maintain a "nuclear stalemate," in spite of minor quantitative and qualitative differences in the armament of the contenders. The destruction caused by one thermonuclear bomb landing on a large city is so out of proportion to the advantage gained from destroying even a large portion of another nation that a rational decision to begin such a war is highly improbable. The recent statement by General Power that 300 Soviet missiles could wipe out our entire nuclear retaliatory force (150 ICBMs on SAC installations and 150 IRBMs [Intermediate Range Ballistic Missiles] on targets nearer the Soviet Union) could under certain circumstances be correct. But a theoretical Soviet capability does not add up to an inevitable eventuality. In the first place, there is no real evidence that the Soviet Union intends to launch such an attack as soon as it is able. Moreover, such a mass, coordinated, split-

[2] In 1952 I heard General Thomas Power, present commanding general of the Strategic Air Command, make the following remark, in substance : "One of SAC's major difficulties is the inability to choose its equipment. A businessman can choose from several different products. But we simply have no choice. Right now SAC is trying to do its job using two airplanes [the B-50 and the B-36], one laid down in 1939 and the other in 1941. If we don't use these, we've got nothing."

second operation would have to be carried out with almost no malfunctions. If only a few missiles failed in flight, or were late being fired, or missed their targets by greater than anticipated distances, the Soviet Union would be open to unacceptable return destruction from that portion of the U.S. retaliatory force not destroyed as planned. Continuous airborne alert by some of SAC's long-range bombers, plus the gradual addition to the American retaliatory force of the Polaris missile-firing nuclear submarines could insure at least a marginal deterrent during the period of the much-discussed "missile gap" of the early 1960s. Attainment of operational capability by the Minuteman "hardened" missile bases,[3] and further development of such air-to-surface missiles as the Hound Dog, fired from long-range aircraft cruising hundreds of miles from the target, will strengthen this retaliatory, or second-strike, capability.

The result is that probably neither the United States nor the Soviet Union will launch a surprise attack against the other in the foreseeable future, not for humanitarian reasons but because of the likely disastrous consequences. Most future strategic plans for the United States, and undoubtedly for the Soviet Union, involve variations of this ability to release a devastating second-strike after taking a surprise first strike. Use of the following techniques, plus others, will contribute to such a retaliatory capability: dispersal (making necessary a great number of enemy weapons fired in order to cover all of the targets), "hardening" (requiring even greater accuracy and actual cratering in order to make sure of the target), and mobility (making it difficult for a missile to zero in on a known "fixed address"). Various combinations of the capabilities of manned aircraft, orbiting satellites, air-to-surface missiles,[4] long-range submarines, and surface-to-surface missiles, with less and less reaction time, even to the macabre "button pushed by a dead man's

[3] A "hardened" base is one which has been buried underground beneath a hard covering such as reinforced concrete to protect it from enemy fire.

[4] Serious development is under way, for example, for the Air Force's CAMAL (Continuous Airborne Missile Alert) and Dynasoar, described as "an unpowered glider, boosted to near satellite speeds and altitudes by rocket engines from which it glides or skips around the earth on the fringes of the atmosphere."

hand," would seem to make the outlook for effective defense almost hopeless for the predictable future.

In spite of earlier statements made here concerning the dominance of superpowers, the possibility cannot be ignored that a nuclear war could be set off by one of the lesser powers. This possibility constitutes a fourth peculiar characteristic of the present international situation. Lesser powers can attain a technological capability which under certain circumstances could be devastating to any other nation on earth. (In current jargon, this is the "Nth Country problem.") We have said that such a decision in favor of nuclear war could not rationally be made. The fact remains that not all political actions are rational. Desperation and miscalculation, coupled with the potentialities latent in surprise and a compact warhead, might have fateful consequences. The "suitcase atomic bomb," for example, is already a technological possibility. Delivery of several such bombs by innocent-appearing agents would not be inconceivable.

The net effect of what we have said is that, if the United States puts its faith in technology alone, there can be no cessation of the terror. The terror will continue as long as the arms race continues, and the arms race will continue until technology is brought under control. The American dilemma is acute: on the one hand, the consequences of allowing the Soviet Union a clear military superiority might well be disastrous; on the other hand, the arms race is an ever-accelerating ordeal which can at any moment precipitate a war of mass destruction. Reason demands that a way out of the dilemma be found; the human mind cannot indefinitely confront two such dreadful alternatives.

If American national security is to be safeguarded, and yet the likelihood of an all-out nuclear war reduced, two conditions would seem to be necessary: 1) American military strategy must be keyed to the realities of the present world political and military situation, so that it will be prepared effectively to counter probable military threats, and yet will not unnecessarily endanger world peace by making military counters to threats which are not military but political or economic. 2) Military technology, tactics and strategy must be brought under control so that the trend toward ever-greater destructiveness is altered, and effective military means are devised to fight wars without threatening the entire fabric of society.

Current Military Strategy

It goes without saying that since the close of World War II the United States has been primarily concerned with only one probable military opponent — the Soviet Union. Even when the immediate adversary in a specific instance has been some other political entity, the Soviet shadow in the background has always constituted the major military concern. Further, since the close of World War II the United States has followed one dominant military strategy. Its chief doctrinal concept has been that of deterring a major Soviet attack through the threat of strategic bombing.

When World War II ended, the Soviet Union was a land power. Its navy was not significant, its tactical air force (organized in air "regiments") was under the control of ground commanders, and its so-called "strategic air force" was chiefly for show and had little capability and less operational experience. The great preponderance of Soviet military attention was devoted to the means by which Russia had met every threat in its history — a land army. The only probable Soviet military action, therefore, was against Western Europe and the Middle East. The only practical American defense, in fact, the only means by which the United States could effectively "get at" its opponent, was by strategic bombing of the Soviet homeland. This strategy was possibly successful in deterring an all-out Soviet attack. We shall probably never know for sure. But it is certain that the Soviets were not greatly intimidated. The period of their greatest intransigence coincided with that of American strategic supremacy.

In spite of the strictures heaped on strategic bombing, the policy was not in itself immoral, at least until it included the air-transportable H-bomb. There were enough primarily military and relatively isolated industrial targets for the strategy to be susceptible of both effective and moral application. I say the policy of strategic bombing was not *in itself* immoral, even though its practice in much of World War II was immoral. The bombing of cities themselves, for the possible effect on civilian morale and destruction of the "will to fight," had already become an accepted portion of Allied air strategy. B. H. Liddell Hart, the noted British military writer, has commented in his *Revolution in Warfare* on the early changes in American and British manuals on the rules of warfare that declared "an attacking force is under no legal duty to limit the bombardment." This Allied military concept was followed even in the face of a pre-war proposal by the Germans to limit attacks on cities. As Liddell Hart states: "The Germans' departure from this code can hardly be dated before September, 1940, when the night bombing of London was launched, following upon six successive attacks on Berlin during the previous fortnight. The Germans were thus strictly justified in describing this as a reprisal, especially as they had, prior to our sixth attack on Berlin, announced that they would take such action if we did not stop our night bombing of Berlin." This is not to imply that the Nazis were more humane than the Allies, such a proposition would be a historical absurdity. But the Allies did carry the policy of strategic bombing to the greatest lengths. H. M. S. Crossman has declared: ". . . the only nations which applied the theory of un-limited war really systematically were the British and Americans, with their gigantic strategic air forces. The Nazis and the Communists dabbled in terror raids on civilian targets. But they were old-fashioned and imperialist enough to hold that the aim of war is not to destroy the enemy but to defeat his armies in the field, to occupy his country, and to plunder its resources." The Allies, on the other hand, explicitly and with full public approval set about pulverizing the enemy's cities. Perhaps influenced by the American experience of "total war" and "unconditional surrender" in their own Civil War, the winning side proceeded to destroy the homes, the families and the future means of livelihood of the losers. The policy of oblitera-tion bombing has reached its ultimate in the strategy of massive re-taliation with H-bombs.

The question of the rights of the civilian sector is again raised by the NATO strategy for "holding" Western Europe in the event of a Soviet attack. This strategy, since 1954, has explicitly been based upon the tactical use of nuclear weapons. Such a strategy is, of course, by no means in itself immoral. Very small atomic weapons can be limited to a blast damage area of a few hundred yards and a fallout area of not much more. They do not have to be used on civilian targets. But here again actual military practice does not give one much confidence.

Today the people of industrialized countries live in conditions which are extremely vulnerable to disruption. In many cases it would be necessary only to fracture this social and economic structure to cause widespread death and suffering. Under such circumstances, one must regard the possibilities of a tactical nuclear war in Western Europe with considerable misgiving. In May, 1956, Hanson Baldwin wrote as follows after attending Operation Sagebrush, maneuvers held to test atomic tactics:

NATO's basic strategy for the defense of Western Europe is based upon a nuclear concept; we will use, it is said, tactical A-weapons to bomb enemy airfields, troops, supply dumps, and other "military" targets. In a thickly settled area like Western Europe this is a stultifying and self-defeating strategy, for no such large-scale tactical nuclear war in this heavily industrialized, heavily populated region could be limited.

It is thoughts such as these which have jellied the backbone of the European alliance and raised serious doubts regarding American military strategy, not only in its threat of massive retaliation but in its basic premises for "defense of the West." Gordon Craig commented on Operation Carte Blanche, a tactical exercise held in Germany in June, 1955:

The only people intimidated by Carte Blanche were the Germans. With a little judicious advance publicity, this might have been avoided. As it was, the first news the Germans had of Carte Blanche came in German newspaper reports that 335 atomic bombs had been "dropped" in the crowded space between Hamburg and Munich, and that — according to unofficial calculation — 1,700,000 Germans had been "killed" and 3,500,000 "wounded," not counting possible casualties from radiation. These alarming figures began to appear in highly colored press accounts in July, when a not very enthusiastic Bundestag was being asked to take the first step toward raising the new German army by passing a bill authorizing the recruitment of six thousand volunteers.

The chief difficulty is that modern tactical wars are not fought in isolated areas, with the civilians roped off like spectators at a knightly tourney. Modern armies completely take over their civilian environment. They house themselves and their equipment in existing structures. They feed and supply themselves using existing roads, railroads, and seaports. They incorporate existing utilities such as telephone, telegraph, power, water, etc. into their operational and logistical systems. Even if one adversary elected to abstain from these advantages, he could not make his enemy do so. In 1954 the "New Look" in American strategy for Western Europe specifically substituted tactical nuclear weapons for the manpower which was no longer anticipated to be available to deter a Soviet attack. This is still our NATO strategy. However, a hard-fought "retreat to the Pyrenees", using nuclear weapons all the way, would probably lay in ruins the nations we are "defending." Surely it would be somewhat fatuous to declaim too loudly that the Europeans do not appreciate all we are doing for them.

Possibly it would be well here to make explicit a point which has been implicit so far. If the United States goes to war with the Soviet Union in the foreseeable future, nuclear weapons will be the "conventional" method of warfare.

As long ago as 1954 Lord Montgomery made the following unequivocal statement regarding NATO's strategy: "I want to make it absolutely clear that we at SHAPE are basing all our operational planning on using atomic and thermonuclear weapons in our defense. It is no longer a question of 'they may possibly be used.' It is very definitely 'they will be used — if we are attacked.'"

In 1957 the secretary of defense, Charles E. Wilson, told an appropriations subcommittee of the House of Representatives:

Our basic defense policy is based on the use of atomic weapons in a major war and is based on the use of such atomic weapons as would be militarily feasible and usable in a smaller war, if such a war is forced upon us.

In other words, the smaller atomic weapons, the tactical weapons, in a sense have now become conventional weapons. There is no such thing as a nice, easy-going war.

47

In the same year Marshal Zhukov emphasized that the Soviet Union was expecting any future major war to be fought with nuclear weapons: "In the event of a major armed clash atomic weapons will inevitably be used as the principal means of offense."

These statements are not idle bluffs. All evidence indicates the Soviet Union is extending tactical atomic training to the lowest levels in its army units, in addition to incorporating nuclear war-heads into its intermediate and long-range missiles. In the United States, all the Army's fourteen divisions have been reorganized, with an atomic capability; though we may well doubt the extent of this capability in terms of actual back-up quantities of small nuclear weapons. Our Air Force operational plans are forthrightly built on the use of nuclear weapons for both tactical and strategic missions. Some of the major tasks of our Navy, such as antisubmarine warfare and deterrence through the threat of Polaris missile submarines, become much more difficult without nuclear weapons. The entire missile program, in fact, makes little sense without nuclear warheads. As President Eisenhower stated four years ago: "One without the other is rather useless." A two-million-dollar missile with a TNT warhead could have difficulty doing two-million-dollars' worth of damage to an industrial target, particularly when the CEP (Circular Error Probability) is considered. In the light of such considerations, it may be gravely doubted whether the United States can ever again fight a major "conventional" war.

There is another type of military strategy, for which the United States is currently being asked to increase its capability. This is the strategy of limited war. There is undoubtedly much political and military knowledge and much good will in the arguments of the limited-war advocates. But the chief difficulty is that the term has been used so often by so many different people to mean so many different things that it has almost lost the capacity to communicate an idea. The chief measure of agreement among all the proponents of limited war seems to be that the war would not be allowed to become an all-out nuclear one. But the term has been also used to connote limitations on geographical area of conflict, type of targets to be hit, number of participating nations, size of forces, kind of weapons to be used, and political objectives to be sought.

A common setting given the term is that of a "peripheral' or "brushfire" war in some Asian or African country where an estab-lished government, friendly to the West, is being attacked in force by revolutionaries who have communist support. According to this theory the United States would airlift to the spot a division (more or less) of special troops who would put down the rebellion and "save" the area for the West. It may well be that the United States should be prepared to fight such wars. But before we put into effect a "Monroe Doctrine for the world," such matters as the following should be publicly and responsibly considered: *1*) The war may not stay small, if the other side really wants to win it. (The Korean War was a small war only by comparison with World War II which preceded it and World War III which it was hoped it would not turn into.) *2*) The war may last a long time. (A modern French army of a half-million men has been tied down in Algeria for over five years; an-other French army spent an even longer time in Indochina before being finally defeated. There is no assurance that even tactical nu-clear weapons would have altered these results. *3*) Peoples of the underdeveloped countries have not welcomed Western military forces even when they themselves were anticommunist. (The rela-tionship between American "gunboat diplomacy" and anti-Ameri-canism in Latin America should be a constant reminder of the ill will created by disregard for a nation's self respect.) *4*) American capability to react to such situations could be easily exhausted if some central directing authority decided to start seven or eight "brushfire" wars at once. The Army's three "strategic" divisions, or even five or six, could be tied down in frustrating protracted conflicts in which they "could hear a breech-bolt snick where never a man was seen." Revolutionary armies need little formal logistical and admin-istrative structure when — as in China, Indochina, Malaya, Algeria, Cuba, and Laos — they strike and fade away into a sympathetic peasantry.

This is not to say that the United States needs no such mobile and even conventional capability. Undoubtedly there will be situations where such forces are required. But, just as with massive retaliation, too much should not be glibly claimed for the strategy. Again as with massive retaliation (or closing the missile gap, for that matter) a limited-war capability of the type described above could well turn out to be another mirage — entrancing from a distance, laborious and expensive to attain, and devoid of practical substance when inexorable reality calls it to account.

The Problem for Future Military Strategy

In sum, American military technology in its pursuit of destructiveness and speed of delivery systems has led American military strategy into a dangerously rigid position. Where this strategy takes the form of massive retaliation, it could not, if put into practice, accomplish its stated purpose or any other rational or moral one. For there can be no doubt that we would be unable to retaliate massively if the Soviet Union decided to launch an all-out nuclear assault on SAC. We would be lucky to be able to retaliate at all. The simple fact is that our capacity for massive retaliation is a first-strike capability, not retaliatory or second-strike. But an even graver indictment of this strategy can be made, and again on purely military grounds. SAC is slowly losing the ability to accomplish a major portion of its mission, even as a first-strike force. It can no longer be denied that we fell behind the Soviet Union in missile development. And we may not be catching up. As the Soviets disperse, harden, and/or make mobile their missile launching sites, destruction of their striking power becomes less and less a statistically valid objective. More and more, therefore, our strategy will become like that of a desperate person holding a bomb in an apartment building: "Don't touch me or I'll blow us all up."

There is a yet further, and still practical, indictment of massive retaliation. The strategy does not meet the time-honored test of "acceptability in its consequences." Nowhere have I seen a careful, matter-of-fact analysis of the consequences of massive retaliation, if the strategy should succeed. What would American policy be if we actually destroyed the social and economic foundation of the

Soviet Union, leaving fifty or seventy-five million people dead and millions more sick and radiation-damaged, without the means to feed themselves, heal themselves, maintain order, or govern themselves? We rebuilt a shattered Germany after World War II: not so much out of charity but because of the impractical consequences of allowing millions of people to become completely desperate and vengeful. If we destroyed the Soviet Union we would probably have to help re-build it. The cost in dollars alone, to mention nothing else, would be fantastic.

Is there, then, no place for the SAC, the Polaris submarines, the ICBMs and IRBMs? Of course there is. The technological clock cannot be set back. From a military standpoint we may well find ourselves in a position where these weapons are the only effective means for bringing force to bear on the Soviet Union. But it is not necessary that all possible destructiveness be crammed into strategic delivery systems, nor that cities and economic installations be targets.

Let us go back in history a little. Throughout World War I, and through much of World War II, a fundamentally different strategic situation existed from that of today. World War I was, in effect, a great "head-to-head shoving contest." Firepower could be concentrated offensively only by massing armies of individuals, with each soldier carrying or otherwise tending a relatively small bit of firepower. The sheer logistical problem of feeding and equipping these armies meant that the nation which first faltered economically, after years of intense effort and slow strangulation, would begin to lose the war. A nation's "war potential" could, then, be crippled by attacks on its ability to produce. But war potential today exists in a completely different form. Firepower cannot only be concentrated; it can be stored and kept in being, ready to use. Slow economic strangulation becomes irrelevant. Thus, civilian and economic targets are today of little immediate military use.

This is not to say that economic targets have lost all significance. In a so-called "broken-backed" war, for example, which according to some writers would proceed on a more or less conventional basis after both sides had exhausted their long-range nuclear capabilities, slow economic attrition would theoretically become effective again.

51

But this kind of convulsive Götterdämmerung assumes a situation wherein almost all worthwhile values have already been destroyed, including, probably, the major economic ones. Even in the Cold War, however, it must be admitted that the threat to civilian and economic targets, in a strategy of massive retaliation, does have a certain deterrent utility. The leaders of the Soviet Union cannot look with indifference at the possibility of even one thermonuclear bomb bursting upon a Soviet city.

When the amoral nature of communist political philosophy is considered, there can be no question that the United States needs something more than promises of "mutual good faith" for a guarantee of security. While it is to be doubted if the Soviets have ever put their trust in the military value of obliteration bombing to the same extent as the Western Allies, the American position will certainly be much safer if it is reinforced by a purely military deterrent which promises the U.S.S.R. unacceptable return damage if it should dare a surprise attack. But if this is our primary need, then American deterrent strategy should be geared directly to this objective, and should not try to accomplish several tasks at once. Our present strategy of massive retaliation aims first at deterring a Soviet all-out attack, then secondly, if the deterrent fails, at "blunting" (reducing the effectiveness of) the Soviet long-range offensive capability, and lastly at destroying other military-industrial-civilian targets which contribute to the ability of the Soviet Union to continue a war. More loosely, there is also sometimes claimed for the strategy of massive retaliation a capability to deter minor forms of communist aggression anywhere in the world. This latter claim is usually made by civilian, rather than military, partisans; it is, moreover, the more enthusiastic versions of this claim which have produced the greatest quantity of criticism for the strategy in general.

We shall disregard entirely this last claim for massive retaliation. It is doubtful if the American military themselves would be in favor of initiating all-out war directly with the Soviet Union over a "brushfire" in Southeast Asia. But the other objectives of massive retaliation listed above are current military doctrine. They have been overtaken by events in the past decade, and they are now becoming technologically obsolete. *1*) The strategy of terror as a deterrent is worthless if the Soviet leaders ever feel that we cannot or will not carry it through. The more the strength and probability of a Soviet counterretaliation increases, the more certain it becomes that the American strike force will be used only in the last resort. If this last resort (a Soviet nuclear attack on the United States) is unlikely to occur, as has been suggested here, then increasingly our primary military strategy is directed toward the least likely military eventuality. *2*) We cannot blunt the Soviet nuclear striking power to a point acceptable to the United States; and our capability in this respect will gradually become less and less. *3*) Economic and industrial targets are militarily of little value, for they do not harbor that portion of the Soviet war potential which is our primary fear — the proliferating missiles and their nuclear warheads, increasingly dispersed, hidden, and mobile.

The United States needs a real deterrent; one which will constitute a tangible threat to the Soviet Union and yet which would be a sound, credible and morally justifiable course of action if it actually had to be put into effect. For such a deterrent, long-range bombers and submarines, coupled with missiles and small nuclear weapons, will undoubtedly be required. But we do not need nuclear weapons of megaton size, with their tremendous blast-areas and fallout that is world-wide. We do not need to think in terms of targets which are primarily civilian in nature or which contribute to the ability of the Soviet Union to fight a long war. If the purpose is to deter, then the United States could announce beforehand that it will destroy with precise nuclear weapons, from secure retaliatory locations, certain targets of as great value as possible to the Soviet Union, but with a minimum impact on the civilian population.

The American military's dedication to destructiveness and speed of delivery systems has perverted our thinking about tactical wars as well as our plans for striking directly at the Soviet Union. Starting with the premise that Western Europe must be held, we have developed a strategy which casts doubt on European civilization's surviving the holding. We have ignored the fact that the day of wars for mere acreage is past. Nations fight today to preserve, or impose

53

on someone else, social, economic, and political systems. If the systems should die in the process of being saved, the real purpose of the war is questionable.

American troops are not in Europe to throw back a Soviet assault. The success of such a venture, for a few divisions at the far end of a three-thousand mile, transoceanic, logistical pipeline, may be considered doubtful. Our troops are in Europe as an earnest of American intention to go to war, if necessary, to defend the area against overt attack, and to assist local governments against the possibility of paramilitary coups by internal, communist-supported forces. Such functions do not require the same military forces, or the same strategies, as the holding of a line against an all-out westward assault by a great land power.

Here, again, a strategy is required which will fit the existing situation in Europe. On the one hand, the Soviet Union must not be allowed to commit aggression with impunity nor to subvert legitimate governments supported by the majority of their people. The existing NATO strategy of "sword and shield" is clearly applicable here. But the deterrent sword must be a practical military weapon and not a flaming sword of terror which is militarily irrelevant to its intended use. And the shield must not pretend that it can defend Europe by itself, and threaten the nuclear destruction of the countries being defended.

Small nuclear weapons undoubtedly have an important place in tactical wars, so long as they can be used without laying waste to the civilian sector. The technological clock can no more be turned back in this respect than it can in strategic operations. But there are some parts of the world where the highly vulnerable nature of the social and economic structure rules out the indiscriminate exchange of nuclear weapons. Much of Western Europe (and the more crowded parts of Asia and Africa) would seem to fall in this category. A strategy is required for tactical wars, therefore, which will not face the United States with the alternatives of either destroying the existing civilization or abandoning it to an aggressor. An integral portion of this strategy would be the use of a deterrent capable of destroying, by means of nuclear weapons and long-range delivery systems, military targets primarily and selected political and even economic ones, in some cases — in the country committing the aggression. This strategy might well be coupled with ultimatums and prior warnings, in some instances.

That aspect of current American strategy which proposes to speed conventional forces to Asian and African "brushfire" wars is also subject to technological (and political) limitations. The entire nature of such wars has changed in the last two decades, yet the change has been largely ignored. Mao Tse-tung and other revolutionary leaders know much more about the new tactics than the professors at West Point, Sandhurst, and Saint Cyr. What is more, these revolutionaries have been winning their wars. They do not fight battles until they are ready. They may not even fight at all. They can afford to wait, for years, if necessary, with only an occasional hacked-up sentry, bombed café, blown bridge, or ambushed convoy to help them keep their hands in. Tanks, airplanes, and artillery are of only limited effectiveness in such wars, so long as the revolutionaries have broad popular support. And they will have popular support until the social, economic, and political inequities in their countries are corrected. America cannot afford to invalidate its vast international aid programs by too rashly participating in local civil wars and thereby incurring the animosity of impoverished peoples.

These "brushfire" wars require a strategy which does not place the United States in the position either of doing nothing or of bogging down a ground army for years in combat with an opponent who will not fight battles and yet will not make peace. Conventional military forces and additional airlift will certainly be needed for some of these emergencies, but an unselfish and forward-looking foreign policy will be much more important.

The fact must be faced that no area can be held for the West if it does not want to be held. The only way to insure that the greater portion of a nation as opposed to an oligarchic governing group, wishes to align itself with the West is to demonstrate that the Western powers have the genuine welfare of the nation at heart. America's primary emphasis, then, should be on economic and technical assistance in alleviating the conditions which might lead to internal conflict. Military assistance in the form of equipment and other indirect aid will often be required, of course, to insure that well-organized armed groups do not take over the nation by force. A corollary of this point would be a refusal by the United States to grant military assistance to governments whose internal policies are repressive and provocative of armed rebellion. Where a nation friendly to the West is overtly attacked by a neighboring country, as happened in Korea, then the situation should be treated as any other tactical war. The primary emphasis should be on carrier-based air-power or any other available method of applying pin-point pressure on selected military and economic targets with minimal impact on the civilian population. Where the United States does not have adequate carrier or land-based air and missile power available, then the situation must be forthrightly faced that there are some portions of the earth's surface beyond the effective reach of American military force.

The chief burden of all that has been said so far is that the United States is ill prepared to meet its potential military problems with effective military solutions. The military and civilian technicians, in their quest for superior destructiveness and speed of delivery, have concentrated on forms of war which vitiate the objectives nations have traditionally sought. Operational military leaders of the past like Wellington in Spain, Washington in the American colonies, and Wingate in Burma — yes, and Mao Tse-tung in China — would never have selected for their campaigns weapons and strategies which completely stultified any rational political objectives. Yet today we find ourselves in a situation where the political objective of any particular strategy is almost ignored in the hectic race to produce the weapons with which the war might be fought.

Destructiveness in a warhead, and speed and range in a delivery system, are not objectives in themselves. These capabilities must contribute to some rational military and political purposes which extend beyond the immediate destruction of the enemy. A deterrent strategy, to be rational, must have implicit within it the intention of being used. If it is used, it must contain a reasonable promise of improving the military position of the user. This improved military position must, if it should become a victorious one, contribute to the furtherance of political purposes which are conducive to the future well-being of mankind.

Present American strategies will not meet these tests. As Secretary of Defense McElroy had admitted in the statement quoted at the beginning of this article, the United States is moving into a period of increasing danger not only for itself but for the people of all the world. Whatever the responsibility of other nations, it is up to the United States to turn its attention from the hypnotic attraction of weapons which promise greater destruction delivered more rapidly over greater distances, and to devise strategies which do not endanger the very values it hopes to defend.

chapter IV

Morality and Security:
The Forgotten Equation*

by Thomas E. Murray

THE CHRISTIAN effort at peace-making, from its origin, undertook the task of civilizing warfare. It set itself against pacifism: the notion that war is always immoral. But it set itself even more strongly against barbarism: the notion that the use of armed force is not subject to any moral restraints. Against these two extremes tradition asserts that war can be a moral action, but only if it is limited in its purposes and methods by the norms of justice.

The fact today is that the Christian tradition of civilized warfare has been ruptured. The chief cause of the rupture has been the doctrine of total war fought to total victory: the kind of victory that looks to the total ruin of the enemy nation. This doctrine of totalization of war represents a regression toward barbarism. It is contrary to the central assertion of the civilized tradition that the aims of war are limited, and the use of force in war is likewise limited, not merely by political and military counsels of expediency, but primarily by the moral principle of justice.

* Originally prepared as an address before the Catholic Association for International Peace, Washington, D.C., November 10, 1956.

The Drift into Barbarism

I need not trace the history of the rupture of this civilized tradition; many doubtless know it better than I. The "patriotism" of the French Revolution gave birth to the concept of "the nation in arms," which led to the idea of universal military conscription. Our own Civil War foreshadowed the fatal notion that "victory" in war means "unconditional surrender." A further step through the concept of total war to total victory was the rejection by the belligerent governments and peoples of Pope Benedict XV's proposals, made on August 1, 1917, for a negotiated peace.

The historically decisive stride in the same direction was taken in World War II by the inception of obliteration bombing. One purpose of this new kind of air attack was to terrorize the enemy civilian population, in particular the industrial worker. The developing logic of total war showed itself in the disastrous announcement at Casablanca in 1943 that "unconditional surrender" was the war aim of the Allied Powers. The immoral decision that the civilian population has no claim to immunity from destruction in war was ratified, with most fearful effectiveness, by the unfortunate American decision to drop atomic bombs on Hiroshima and Nagasaki.

Since World War II the technical possibilities for obliteration bombing have now become unlimited. The United States discovered the secret of the hydrogen bomb; later the Soviet Union came upon the same secret. The significance of this technological achievement cannot be exaggerated. Weapons of war have moved up into a new order of magnitude. Now the barbaric doctrine that "everybody may be killed in war" is assured of its success. Now everybody *can* be killed in war — easily, quickly, cheaply.

Throughout the course of this whole historical development no one has ever made the argument that war ought to be made total, as a matter of reason and right. War simply became more and more total, as a matter of fact and possibility. The immoral impulses of exaggerated nationalism began the development. The material achievements of modern technology completed it. Technological progress has finally removed all the purely circumstantial limitations formerly imposed on warfare: restricted financial resources, difficulties in transport and communications, and, most important, inferior weaponry.

This is the historic juncture at which we now stand. If limitations are to be imposed on warfare today, they can be imposed only by the free decisions of men. No other source of limitation presently exists. This is why we stand at a parting of the ways. Two paths are open. In his encyclical of November 2, 1956, Pope Pius XII called one "the road of justice," and the other "the steep slope of violence."

Man at a Moral Crossroads

Man can choose to let the mad logic of total war dictate his decisions with regard to military policies and weapons programs. This steep slope of violence, followed far enough, leads toward the totality of ruin implicit in the today's technologically certain fact: "Everybody can now be killed in war."

Or man can choose to shake off the hold which this mad logic has fastened upon his mind. He can elect to return to the road of justice: to the civilized tradition of limited warfare. He can recognize that the enterprise of war is inherently subject to certain limitations in its purposes and methods; that these limitations find their original source and their final authority in the moral order; that this order is sanctioned by God; and that its precepts are therefore absolute in their command over all human action, including the action of war.

Only along this path of moral choice, as I shall say, will men find their way to security. In the last analysis, only the principle of justice can draw the line between civilized warfare and sheer massacre, between legitimate defense of the basic order of human life and the barbaric destruction of all order in human life. Unless this line is drawn, with absolute firmness, there can be no solid foundation for human security.

I do not say that it will be easy to draw the line at which the civilian claim to immunity from violence in war asserts itself in the face of the counsels of military expediency. But I do say that this civilian claim is made in the inviolable name of justice and that all

60

military operations — defensive or retaliatory — must respect it. All expediencies cede in the face of justice.

Similarly, I do not maintain that it will be easy to reverse the trend of a century-old regression into the immoral concept of war as total, and to reaffirm the trend of the Christian tradition toward the concept of war as limited. But I do maintain that this task is not impossible. It is always within the power of man to abandon false ideas and to dismantle the institutions built upon them. He can therefore do away with the idea and institution of total war, if only he decides firmly enough that he wants to do so, and that in the nuclear age he must do so.

He has already been powerfully helped to this decision by the facts themselves. On the practical level, the bankruptcy of any policy of total war is today amply evident. A total nuclear war, fought to a total victory, could only mean total woe. It would mean "woe to the vanquished," in a sense far beyond the savage meaning of that barbarian cry. And it would mean woe to the victor too, when he found himself in a world of ruins, amid a humanity which would bear death in its very bones. Here is an argument that must give pause even to the most cynical exponents of violence.

For us, however, the rejection of total war must be more solidly based. Our appeal must be to the high principles of justice that lie at the heart of the Western tradition of civilized warfare. Human reason has never refuted these high principles; the will of man has simply abandoned them. The tradition did not succumb to argument, but only to fact: to the fact of man's passions, as they are aroused by the violence of war, and proceed to arm themselves with the products of technology.

Here perhaps I should note that the reason and moral conscience of America too have been obscured by the dark fires of wartime passion. Upon us too, as upon other nations, there rests a responsibility for the rupture of the tradition of civilized warfare. Not least for this reason there rests upon us a responsibility for repairing the breach.

The principles of the tradition are still with us, in all their un-

61

diminished vitality. The problem is to translate them into practical conclusions in two areas of urgent concern: first, our military policy in general, and second, a weapons program that will support our military policies. The way I see the structure of the problem will be expanded below.

Our Defense Problem

The present goal of all the policies of the United States is to force the conflict with communism out of the field of armed violence into the areas of diplomacy, politics, and economics. These areas are highly competitive indeed; but competition in them does not mean bloodshed. They are the chosen areas in which we undertake to urge the cause of justice for all men. Moreover, we must be continually mindful that the conflict with communism is basically spiritual; therefore, our victory will not be won without recourse to the sword of the spirit which is the word of God.

The primary military contribution toward this general American goal must be the maintenance of the capacity to deter all unjust aggression even of a limited kind. The primacy of this function of force is reinforced today because our principal enemy will be restrained from the use of force only if we convince him that it will prove too costly to him.

This policy of deterrence may fail. Military aggression of one kind or another may occur. Peaceful methods of rectifying the injustice thus committed may likewise fail. We shall then be forced into war. This contingency must be faced now. The problem is to determine, in advance of this contingency, the military policies that will be consistent with the tradition of civilized warfare.

At one extreme, justice requires that we reject the concept of total nuclear warfare. The bald fact that large nuclear bombs can wipe out whole civilian populations does not put an end to the claim of the civilian to immunity from the violence of war.

At the other extreme, our tradition of civilized warfare does not require that we succumb to the deception involved in the Soviet proposal that all use of nuclear weapons be outlawed. This propaganda aims to make the world believe that any use of nuclear weapons inevitably means the totalization of the conflict. This is not true. A nuclear war can still be a limited war. To believe otherwise is to deny that man is a rational being capable of controlling his own actions. It is likewise to assert that American military men are incapable of making intelligently moral use of their new weapon.

Furthermore, in the present situation of international lawlessness a total renouncement of nuclear armaments by the United States would mean the betrayal of our moral tradition, which requires that we should not abandon the cause of justice or leave ourselves unprepared to defend it effectively.

Both of these extremes contain the moral fallacy of totalization. Between them we must find a middle course, the road of justice. It leads to a firmly defined but flexible military policy that will recognize two principles as controlling in the use of nuclear arms: first, the military principle of necessity or usefulness, and second, the higher moral principle of justice in the use of force.

This brings me to the next question. It is the practical question of developing a nuclear weapons program which will be consistent with the foregoing general military policies.

Here I want to lay all possible emphasis on the initial principle that our military policies must control our weapons program. The fatal error that we are presently in danger of making is that of allowing weapons to dictate policy. The danger is really twofold — first, that we allow weapons technology to control the weapons program; and second, that we allow the stockpiled results of the weapons program to control military policies with regard to the use of the stockpile. To succumb to these related dangers would be to turn the whole of U.S. policy upside down.

Rational Nuclear Armament

In April, 1956, I outlined a nuclear weapons program that would avert these dangers and give to moral principles and military policies their proper primacy over weapons. To the program I gave the title, "rational nuclear armaments." There were three proposals.

The first concerned the size of thermonuclear bombs. Three considerations led me to my position. I stated the first in a speech given

63

on November 17, 1955, when I said that the advent of the H-bomb "taught us, not only that the we had a new weapon, but that we had a different kind of weapon. . . . The thermonuclear bomb crosses the threshold into a separate category of power."

The second consideration, closely related to the first, is the fact that it is technologically possible to enlarge indefinitely the qualitatively new dimension of destructiveness created by the hydrogen bomb. I adverted to this fact in a statement before the Senate Subcommittee on Disarmament on April 12, 1956, in these words: "We know that there is no upper limit to the size of bombs that can be made. . . ."

The third consideration is likewise something that we know. As I put it in the November, 1955, speech, already cited: ". . . there is a limit to the number of large thermonuclear explosions that the human race can withstand without harmful bodily effect" consequent on radioactive products.

From these three considerations a conclusion follows. We ourselves must make a responsible decision with regard to the size of H-bombs that we undertake to manufacture. This decision is not only technological and military, but also moral. It must be controlled by the moral principle of justice as well as by the military principle of usefulness. My proposal was that we make this imperative decision, setting an upper limit to the size of H-bombs to be placed in stockpile. I have already given it as my conviction that the weapons we have in hand are large enough. Indeed, they may prove to be too large. Once we make this decision regarding size we can be free to give attention to the problem of improving the deliverability and consequently the military usefulness of weapons in the range up to this limit. In addition, we should set a limit to the number, as well as to the size, of the large weapons that we accumulate. The reason is the presumption that there are only a limited number of uses, militarily and morally justifiable, to which the large bombs might be put.

My second proposal was that we concentrate increasingly on the development of nuclear weapons in the lower order of destructiveness and that we equip ourselves with a wide range of weapons in this order. The purpose of this policy is to strengthen our capabilities

64

for waging all the kinds of limited warfare into which we may possibly be forced.

Thirdly, I came to the question of tests. Recently there has been much debate concerning the hazards to health involved in past and continued testing of large nuclear weapons. This is an area in which at the present time a great deal of uncertainty exists. My proposals, however, are not based on these considerations. They follow from the two major policy decisions I have recommended. My proposals are, first, no tests should be held of weapons whose magnitude would exceed the upper limit which we must set to the size of our nuclear weapons. Second, we should accelerate the testing of a wide range of weapons in the lower order of nuclear force. The reason is that our objective should be a balanced stockpile, suited to every strategic and tactical need, but confined within the bounds set by justice to the use of force.[1]

The weapons program I proposed is rational in two senses. It is consistent with the moral principles of the civilized tradition, and it is adapted to the military necessities of the nuclear age.

One further comment needs to be made. My proposals for a rational weapons program have to be considered as a structured unit, consistent in itself and in its premises.

The program that I propose is designed to carry us through the

[1] [Editor's note: This paragraph is still substantially representative of Mr. Murray's position on testing of nuclear weapons. In the four years that have passed since he first publicly made this proposal, he has refined his position to provide for the complete elimination of atmospheric testing of weapons of *any* size. He has urged that necessary tests of small weapons be conducted underground. In a report to the Chairman of the Joint Congressional Committee on Atomic Energy, titled "The Present United States Ban on Nuclear Testing," and dated May 8, 1959, Mr. Murray maintained that the "security of the United States and the Free World" demands "an intensive test program of lower kiloton and fractional kiloton weapons for essential military purposes." He continued: "This test program can be conducted underground. Therefore it will entail no radioactive contamination of the atmosphere and no hazards to world health from fallout. We have already developed the techniques for controlling and containing dangerous radioactive products from underground explosions. The techniques can be further perfected. On the other hand, tests conducted within the earth's atmosphere, from which contamination and fallout result, are presently not an essential demand of military security. We can afford to forego this manner of testing." See also Mr. Murray's recently published book *Nuclear Policy for War and Peace* (Cleveland and New York: The World Publishing Company, 1960).]

critical era of uncertain duration which confronts us. The crisis concerns, at bottom, the nature of man. But by the same token, it concerns the nature of war, as a human action. The danger in the crisis is that we commit ourselves to the steep violence that ends in the abyss. But let us not overlook the opportunity which the crisis likewise presents: the great historic opportunity to choose the road of justice, and to undertake the restoration of the tradition of civilized warfare.

It is with a view to grasping this opportunity that I put forward my program for rational nuclear armament. Its several proposals are counsels of strength, not of weakness. But the strength they counsel is both military and moral. Therefore they constitute a program for security in the present crisis. They recognize that the security of America does not reside solely in its military power but more basically in its moral strength; the kind of strength that ultimately controls the use of power, and makes it serve the ends of justice.

Morality and Security

Our national and international security has been undermined today largely by the rupture of the tradition of civilized warfare. This, and not the discovery of atomic energy, lies at the root of the terror experienced by the world at the thought of war. There will be no security as long as the rupture of the tradition endures. We shall have no security as long as we are prisoners of the moral fallacy of totalization; that is, as long as we consent to the immoral notion of total war, as long as we dream of the impossible notion of total victory, and as long as we cherish the empty illusion that our national security is totally reposed in massive military might. These fallacies furnish the impulse toward the steep slope of violence.

A program of rational nuclear armament would go far toward rescuing us from these disastrous fallacies. In setting us on the road of justice it would likewise set us on the road to security.

A balanced stockpile, resting on a broad base of small atomic weapons, would not indeed be the most destructive stockpile that we are capable of producing. It would not contain the increasingly immense weapons that the United States could manufacture, if we wanted, but that we could not use without carrying the enterprise of warfare over that fixed line, drawn by the principles of justice, which divides civilized warfare from barbarism. Moreover, the kind of stockpile I propose would not be the cheapest that could be assembled; it would not equip us to deal out the greatest number of deaths for the least number of dollars.

But for my part, I reject the reckless line of thought which would identify our national security with the accumulation of the most destructive possible nuclear arsenal and the cheapest possible nuclear arsenal. This kind of armament, heavily overweighted on the side of megaton bombs, would make neither military nor moral sense. It would not strengthen our military position in the face of threats from the Soviet Union or from other sources. Still less would it buttress our moral standing in the eyes of the international community. On the contrary, it would endanger both. And it would, in consequence, undermine our security.

This brings me to what I call "the forgotten equation." I mean the equation between morality and security. This equation is inherent in the Western tradition. The first security that a civilized nation must protect is the security of its own moral life. The nation is secure in proportion to its fidelity to the moral norms that form the spiritual substance of the national life. Concretely, if the United States is obliged to have recourse to armed force in its own defense, it must understand that it is committed to a moral use of force, on penalty of self-destruction — I mean the destruction of its moral self.

The security which America seeks cannot be simply physical. It must also mean the protection of the spiritual identity of America as a member of the family of civilized nations. If America were to lose its own soul by sins of unjust violence, it matters little what else it might gain.

The tragedy is that in our day this equation between security and morality has been forgotten. We have come to believe that security means only one thing — massive power. And we have forgotten that the methods of power, when used in violation of the canons of justice, will undermine the basic moral security of the whole edifice of civilization which they should undertake to protect.

The equation between morality and security is, I say, part of our tradition. The nuclear age has confronted us with another equation whose ultimate terms are terrible indeed. I mean the equation between the immoral use of nuclear force and the destruction of all human security, even the fundamental security of human life itself. Surely this new equation should serve to jog our memories and bring to mind the old equation that we have forgotten. The reforging of the broken link between morality and security is itself an important element in the restoration of the tradition of civilized warfare.

To this task of restoration we are summoned today by the stringent demand of a moral obligation. It is a duty that we owe to ourselves as a civilized nation. It is further a duty that we owe to Almighty God whose precepts presided over the formation of our constitutional commonwealth.

chapter V

Theology and Modern War*

by John Courtney Murray, S.J.

T HERE ARE three distinct standpoints from which it is possible to launch a discussion of the problem of war in this strange and perilous age of ours that has yet to find its name. My initial assertion will be that it is a mistake to adopt any one of them exclusively and to carry the argument on to its logical conclusions. If this is done, the argument will end in serious difficulties.

First, one might begin by considering the possibilities of destruction and ruin, both physical and human, that are afforded by existent and projected developments in weapons technology. Here the essential fact is that there are no inherent limits to the measure of chaos that war might entail, whether by the use of nuclear arms or possibly by the methods of bacteriological and chemical warfare. Carried to its logical conclusion an argument made exclusively from this standpoint leads toward the position that war has now become a moral absurdity, not to be justified in any circumstances today. In its most

* Originally prepared as an address to the Catholic Association for International peace, October 24, 1958, and subsequently published in *Theological Studies*, 20 (1959), 40–61.

respectable form this position may be called relative Christian pacifism. It does not assert that war is intrinsically evil simply because it is a use of force and violence and therefore a contravention of the Christian law of love promulgated in the Sermon on the Mount. This is absolute pacifism, an unqualified embrace of the principle of nonviolence; it is more characteristic of certain Protestant sects. The relative pacifists are content to affirm that war has now become an evil that may no longer be justified, given the fact that no adequate justification can be offered for the ruinous effects of today's weapons of war. Even this position, I shall say, is not to be squared with the public doctrine of the Church.

Second, one might begin the argument by considering the present historical situation of humanity as dominated by the fact of communism. The essential fact here is that communism, as an ideology and as a power-system, constitutes the gravest possible menace to the moral and civilizational values that form the basis of "the West," understanding the term to designate, not a geographical entity but an order of temporal life that has been the product of valid human dynamisms tempered by the spirit of the Gospel. Arguing from this standpoint alone one could well posit, in all logic, the present validity of the concept of the "holy war." Or one might come to some advocacy of "preventive" war or "pre-emptive" war. Or one might be led to assert that, since the adversary is completely unprincipled, and since our duty in face of him is success in the service of civilization itself, we must jettison the tradition of civilized warfare and be prepared to use any means that promise success. None of these conclusions is morally acceptable.

Third, one might choose as a starting point the fact that today there exists a mode of international organization that is committed by its charter to the preservation of peace by pacific settlement of international disputes. One might then argue that the validity of war even as a legal institution has now vanished, with the passing of the hypothesis under which its legal validity was once defended, namely, the absence of a juridically organized international community. But this conclusion seems, at very best, too rapid, for several reasons.

The United Nations is not, properly speaking, a juridical organization with adequate legal authority to govern in the international community. It is basically a power organization. And its decisions, like those rendered by war itself, are natively apt to sanction injustice as well as justice. It is not at all clear that the existence of the United Nations, as presently constituted, definitely destroys the hypothesis on which the validity of war as a legal institution has traditionally been predicated. It is not at all clear that the United Nations in its present stage of development will be able to cope justly and effectively with the underlying causes of international conflict today or with the particular cases of conflict that may arise.

If therefore one adopts a single standpoint of argument, and adheres to it narrowly and exclusively, one will not find one's way to an integral and morally defensible position on the problem of war. On the other hand, all of the three standpoints mentioned do derive from real aspects of the problem itself. In consequence, each of them must be exploited, if the problem is to be understood in its full scope. This is my second assertion. It is not possible here to develop it in detail. I shall merely suggest that there are three basic questions that must be explored at length and in detail. Moreover, there is an order among these questions.

The Nature of the Conflict

The first question concerns the exact nature of the conflict that is the very definition of international life today. This is the first question because it sets the perspectives in which all other questions must be considered.[1]

I would note here that Pius XII fairly steadily considered the problem of war and of the weapons of war, as well as the problem of international organization, within the perspectives of what he called "the

[1] As a minor contribution to this analysis I attempted a description of the unique character of the Soviet Empire in *Foreign Policy and the Free Society* (New York, 1958), pp. 21–49. In what concerns academic and public opinion in the English-speaking world, a considerable difficulty arises from the fact that there exists no real consensus with regard to the aims and motivations of communist imperialism in its action on the world scene. There are at least four schools of thought; their major difference arises from their variant estimates of the role of ideology in Soviet behavior.

71

line of rupture which divides the entire international community into opposed blocs," with the result that "coexistence in truth" is not possible, since there is no common acceptance of a "norm recognized by all as morally obligatory and therefore inviolable."

I would further note that the exact nature of the international conflict is not easily and simply defined. The line of rupture is not in the first instance geographic but spiritual and moral; and it runs through the West as well as between East and West. It cannot be a question of locating on "our" side of the rupture those who are virtuous and intelligent, and, over against "us," those who are evil and morally blind. In contrast, it cannot be a question of maintaining that both East and West are so full of moral ambiguities that the line of rupture between them either does not exist or is impossible to discern.[2] In a word, one must avoid both a moral simplism and a moral scepticism in the analysis of the international conflict.

Finally, it is most important to distinguish between the mainsprings of the conflict and its concrete manifestations; or, with Sir David Kelly, between the relatively superficial facts of change in our revolutionary world and the underlying currents of change. Moreover, it is important to relate the two levels of analysis, insofar as this can be done without artificiality.

The tendency of this whole line of analysis, bearing on the nature of the international conflict, will be to furnish an answer to a complex of questions that must be answered before it is possible to consider

[2] This view exists in a number of forms. There is, for instance, the contextualistic morality of Prof. Hans Morgenthau, revealed in his Introduction to E. Lefever, *Ethics and United States Foreign Policy* (New York, 1957). His basic view, never quite brought to philosophical explicitness, seems to be that all moralities are purely "national"; they cannot be subjected to judgment in terms of universal principles. There are also various types of neo-Lutheran theory which see evil as radical, ubiquitous, and inextricable in all human action. In quite a different category there are those who are confused, as well they might be in this age, by the problem of the relations between morality and power; cf., for instance, an intelligent and earnest thinker, Mr. Kenneth Thompson, "Moral Choices in Foreign Affairs," *Worldview* (Sept., 1958). One of today's characteristically confused debates goes on between the "realists" and the "idealists." One school holds that politics is wholly a matter of morality; the other maintains that politics is wholly a matter of power. Both are wrong. But they agree on a disastrous tenet, that between morality and power a great gulf is fixed.

the more narrow problems of war. What precisely are the values, in what hierarchical scale, that today are at stake in the international conflict? What is the degree of danger in which they stand? What is the mode of the menace itself — in particular, to what extent is it military, and to what extent is it posed by forms of force that are more subtle? If these questions are not carefully answered, one will have no standard against which to match the evils of war. And terror, rather than reason, will command one's judgments on the military problem. This is the danger to which the seven moral theologians in Germany pointed in their statement of May 5, 1958:

A part of the confusion among our people has its source in the fact that there is an insufficient realization of the reach of values that are endangered today, and of the hierarchical order among them, and of the degree of danger in which they stand. On the other hand, from the *Unheimlichkeit* of the technical problems [of war itself] there results a crippling of intelligence and of will.

The second basic question concerns the means that are available for insuring the defense of the values that are at stake in the international conflict. This too is a large and complex question. A whole array of means is available, in correspondence with the multifaceted character of the conflict itself. It is a matter of understanding both the usefulness and the limitations of each of them, from spectacular "summit meetings" down the gamut to the wholly unspectacular work, say, of agricultural experts engaged in increasing the food supply of so-called "underdeveloped" nations. This whole complex question of the means of conflict must be fully explored antecedently to the consideration of the problem of war. The basic reason is that otherwise one can give no concrete meaning to the concept of war as *ultima ratio*. Moreover, the value of the use of force, even as *ultima ratio*, will be either overestimated or underestimated, in proportion as too much or too little value is attached to other means of sustaining and pressing the international conflict.

The third and final question concerns the *ultima ratio* itself, the arbitrament of arms as the last resort.

Here we confront the third novelty in the total problem. The present historical situation of international conflict is unique. "Never,"

73

said Pius XII, "has human history known a more gigantic disorder."
The uniqueness of the disorder resides, I take it, in the unparalleled
depth of its vertical dimension; it goes to the very roots of order and
disorder in the world — the nature of man, his destiny, and the
meaning of human history. There is a uniqueness too in the second
basic question posited above, sc., the unprecedented scope of the
conflict in its horizontal dimension, given the variety of means
whereby it may be, and is being, waged. A special uniqueness resides
too in the existence of the United Nations, as an arena of conflict
indeed, but also as an instrument of peacemaking to some degree.
However, the most immediately striking uniqueness comes to view
when one considers the weapons for warmaking that are now in hand
or within grasp.

There are two subordinate questions under this general heading of
the nature of war today. The first concerns the actual state of progress (if it be progress and not a regress to barbarism) in the technology of defensive and offensive weapons of war. The second concerns
the military usefulness, for any intelligible military and political
purposes, of the variety of weapons developed. This latter question
raises the issue of the strategic and tactical concepts that are to govern the use of these various weapons. The facts that would furnish
answers to these questions are to a considerable extent hidden from
the public knowledge; and, to the extent to which they are known,
they have been generative of confusion in the public mind. In any
case, these questions must have some reasonably satisfactory answer,
if the moral problem of war is to be sensibly discussed.

Here then are three preliminary lines of inquiry to be pursued
before the moral issues involved in warfare today can be dealt with,
even in their generality.

A Moral Theory

An initial, not necessarily complete, exploration of these three
lines is sufficient to suggest the outlines of a general moral theory.
Whether Catholic thought can be content to stop with a moral
theory cast simply in the mode of abstractness that characterizes the
following propositions will be a further question. In any case, it is

74

necessary in the first instance to state the general propositions. In stating them I am undertaking to render the substance of the thought of Pius XII; but there will be only a minimum of citation, and even of explanation.

1. All wars of aggression, whether just or unjust, fall under the ban of moral proscription.

I use the term "war of aggression" because Pius XII used it.[3] However, he gives no real definition of the term. It seems to stand simply as the contrary of a war of self-defense (whose definition, as we shall see, is more concrete and historical). Expressly, the pope denied that recourse to force is "a legitimate solution for international controversies and a means for the realization of national aspirations." He seems therefore to deny to individual states, in this historical moment, the *jus belli* (*compétence de guerre*) of the modern era of the unlimited sovereign state, sc., the rights of recourse to war, on the sovereign judgment of the national state, for the vindication of legal rights and legitimate interests. The use of force is not now a moral means for the redress of violated legal rights. The justness of the cause is irrelevant; there simply is no longer a right of self-

[3] The concept of aggression is undoubtedly a major source of bedevilment in the whole modern discussion of the problem of war. The recent lengthy attempt to reach a satisfactory definition resulted in failure; cf. Julius Stone, *Aggression and World Order* (Berkeley, Calif., 1958). The concept, I think, is a typically modern one; older theories more characteristically spoke in terms of "injustice." I venture the opinion, merely as an opinion, that the modern prominence of the concept derives from the modern theory that there may be "justice" on both sides of a conflict. Hence the issue of "justice" is proximately decided by "aggression," sc., which nation's armed forces first cross the borders of the other nation. But this military transcription of a basically moral concept is of little, if any, use in our contemporary situation, with its two unique new features. First, today's weapons systems make possible the employment of force at enormous distances without concern for the space between; the concept of "crossing borders" no longer means anything. Second, in view of the striking power of these weapons systems the nation that initiates the attack ("crosses the border") can render the opposing nation defenseless, incapable of exerting a right of self-defense. Consequently, aggression in the older military-moral sense has ceased to be a standard by which to decide the issue of justice in war; it has become simply a technique by which to decide the issue of success. The use of force can no longer be linked to the moral order merely by the concept of aggression, in the modern understanding of the concept. There is urgent need for a thorough moral re-examination of the basic American policy that "we will never shoot first." Under contemporary circumstances, viewed in their entirety, is this really a *dictamen rationis*?

75

redress; no individual state may presume to take even the cause of justice into its own hands. Whatever the grievance of the state may be, and however objectionable it may find the status quo, warfare undertaken on the sovereign decision of the national state is an immoral means for settling the grievance and for altering existent conditions.[4]

If this be the correct interpretation of Pius XII's thought, it will be seen that an important modification of the modern scholastic doctrine of war has been made.[5] The reasons for making it derive from two of the above-mentioned lines of inquiry. First, the immeasurably increased violence of war today disqualifies it as an apt and proportionate means for the resolution of international conflicts and even

[4] Modern theory distinguished three reasons for recourse to war by the sovereign state: *ad vindicandas offensiones, ad repetendas res, ad repellendas injurias*. Pius XII, it seems to me, outlawed the first two categories of "war-aims." The third category is proper to the concept of "defensive" war. At that, the main thrust of his thought on war, viewed in the total context of his dominant concern with international organization, goes against the modern notion of the *jus belli* as an inherent attribute of national sovereignty.

[5] For a statement of the modern scholastic theory, and a critique of it, cf. A. Vanderpol, *La doctrine scolastique du droit de guerre* (Paris, 1919.). It would be interesting to have a new study made of this book, which is not without its bias. I also suggest another question. Pius XII seems relatively unconcerned to give an exact definition of aggression. He seems to want to move back into the center of Catholic thought the older, broader Augustinian concept of *causa justa*. War is not simply a problem of aggression; more fundamentally it is a problem of injustice. It is the concept of justice that links the use of force with the moral order. Would it be correct to say that Pius XII represents an effort to return Catholic thought to more traditional and more fruitful premises? If there is a way out of the present impasse created by the outworn concept of aggression in the modern sense, it can only be a return to the concept of justice. There would still remain the formidable moral and legal problem of translating *justitia* into *tò justum*. In politico-moral terms this is today the problem of what is called "policy." As a moral problem, war is ultimately a problem of policy, and therefore a problem of social morality. Policy is made by society, especially in a democratic context; and society bears the moral responsibility for the policy made. As a problem in justice, the problem of war is put to the People, in whom, according to good medieval theory, the sense of justice resides, and from whom the moral judgment, direction, and correction of public policy must finally come. As a moral problem in the use of force, war is not simply, or even primarily, a problem for the generals, the state department, the technologists, the international lawyers. Here, if anywhere, "the People shall judge." This is their responsibility, to be discharged before the shooting starts, by an active concern with the moral direction of national policy. My impression is that this duty in social morality is being badly neglected in America at the moment.

for the redress of just grievances. Second, to continue to admit the right of war, as an attribute of national sovereignty, would seriously block the progress of the international community to that mode of juridical organization which Pius XII regarded as the single means for the outlawry of all war, even defensive war. In this connection, it would be well to note the observation of M. Gabriel Matagrin: "The preoccupation of Pius XII seems to be much less to determine what might be just in the actual situation of an unorganized humanity than to promote a genuine international organization capable of eliminating war, because the juridical reason for the right of war is the unorganized state of international life."

Pius XII clearly stigmatized "aggressive" war as "a sin, an offense, and an outrage against the majesty of God." Should this sin in the moral order also be transposed into a crime in the legal order? Pius expressly said that "modern total war, and ABC [Atomic-Biological-Chemical] warfare in particular," when it is not stringently in self-defense, "constitutes a crime worthy of the most severe national and international sanctions." [6] I should think that the same recommendation would apply to less violent forms of "aggressive" warfare. However, Pius XII did not enter the formidable technical problem, how this legal transcription of a moral principle is to be effected. The problem has hitherto been insoluble.

2. A defensive war to repress injustice is morally admissible both in principle and in fact.

In its abstractness this principle has always formed part of Catholic doctrine; by its assertion the Church finds a way between false extremes of pacifism and bellicism. Moreover, the assertion itself, far from being a contradiction of the basic Christian will to peace, is the strongest possible affirmation of this will. There is no peace without justice, law, and order. But "law and order have need at times of the powerful arm of force." And the precept of peace itself requires

---

[6] Allocution to the World Medical Congress, Sept. 30, 1954; AAS, 46 (1954), 589. The tradition maintains that the highest value in society is the inviolability of the order of rights and justice. If this order disintegrates or is successfully defied, society is injured in its most vital structure and end. Peace itself is the work of justice; and therefore peace is not compatible with impunity for the evil of injustice. It is pertinent to emphasize these truths in an age in which economic and material values have come to assume the primacy.

77

that peace be defended against violation: "The precept of peace is of divine right. Its purpose is to protect the goods of humanity, inasmuch as they are the goods of the Creator. Among these goods there are some of such importance for the human community that their defense against an unjust aggression is without doubt fully justified."

There is nothing new about these assertions. What is important is their reiteration by Pius XII in today's highly concrete historical context of international conflict. The reiteration of the right of defensive war derives directly from an understanding of the conflict and from a realization that nonviolent means of solution may fail. The Church is obliged to confront the dreadful alternative: "the absolute necessity of self-defense against a very grave injustice that touches the community, that cannot be impeded by other means, that nevertheless must be impeded on pain of giving free field in international relations to brutal violence and lack of conscience."

The harshness of statement in that last phrase marks a new note that came only late (in 1953) into the Pius XII's utterances. I think it fair to say that the gentle Pope of Peace brought himself only with great reluctance, and under the unrelenting pressure of events, to focus on the instant possibility of war, as generated by the essential ethos of the communist system: "brutal violence and lack of conscience." The focus becomes even sharper after the events in Hungary, and in the light of the Soviet threat to use atomic weapons in Europe if the French and English adventure in Suez were not terminated. These words from the Christmas message, 1956, need to be quoted:

The actual situation, which has no equivalent in the past, ought nevertheless to be clear to everyone. There is no further room for doubt about the purposes and the methods that lie behind tanks when they crash resoundingly across frontiers to distribute death and to force civilized peoples to a form of life that they distinctly abhor. When all the possible stages of negotiation and mediation are bypassed, and when the threat is made to use atomic arms to obtain concrete demands, whether these are justified or not, it becomes clear that, in present circumstances, there may come into existence in a nation a situation in which all hope of averting war becomes vain. In this situation a war of efficacious self-defense against unjust attacks, which is undertaken with hope of success, cannot be considered illicit.

One can almost feel the personal agony behind the labored sentences (more tortured in the original than in the translation). The agony, and utterance itself, are born of the pope's reluctant realization that, as he had said earlier that same year, there are rulers "who except themselves from the elementary laws of human society." The tragedy in the situation is accented by his further vision that the people over whom these rulers stand "cannot but be the first to feel the need once more to form part of the human family."

The Conditions of War

There is no indication that this reaffirmation of the traditional principle of defensive warfare, to which Pius XII was driven by the brutal facts of international life, extends only to wars conducted by so-called "conventional" arms. On the contrary, the pope extended it explicitly, not only to atomic warfare but even to ABC warfare. One cannot therefore uphold the simple statement that atomic war as such, without further qualifications, is morally unjustifiable, or that all use of atomic weapons in war is, somehow in principle, evil.

There are, however, conditions. The basic condition has been stated: "One cannot, even in principle, raise the question of the liceity of ABC warfare except in the case in which it must be judged indispensable for self-defense in the conditions indicated." These further conditions are simply those found in traditional doctrine. But each of them was sharpened to a fresh stringency by Pius XII in the light of the horrors of destruction and death now possible in war.

Briefly, the war must be "imposed by an obvious and extremely grave injustice." No minor infraction of rights will suffice, much less any question of national prestige. The criterion is high, namely, that the nation should "in all truth have been unjustly attacked and menaced in its vital rights."

The second condition is the familiar principle of war as always the *ultima ratio*. Moreover, it is today the extremity of means in a unique sense, given, on the one hand, the new means of negotiation and arbitration presently available, and on the other, the depths of manifold agony into which recourse to the *ultima ratio* may now plunge humanity as a whole.

79

The third condition is also familiar, the principle of proportion. It invokes a twofold consideration.

First, consideration must be given to the proportion between the damage suffered in consequence of the perpetration of a grave injustice, and the damages that would be let loose by a war to repress the injustice. Pius XII laid some stress on the fact that the comparison here must be between realities of the moral order, and not sheerly between two sets of material damage and loss. The standard is not a "eudaemonism and utilitarianism of materialist origin," which would avoid war merely because it is uncomfortable, or connive at injustice simply because its repression would be costly. The question of proportion must be evaluated in more tough-minded fashion, from the viewpoint of the hierarchy of strictly moral values. It is not enough simply to consider the "sorrows and evils that flow from war." There are greater evils than the physical death and destruction wrought in war. And there are human goods of so high an order that immense sacrifices may have to be borne in their defense. By these insistences Pius XII transcended the vulgar pacifism of sentimentalist and materialist inspiration that is so common today.

Second, Pius XII required an estimate of another proportion, between the evils unleashed by war and what he called "the solid probability of success" in the violent repression of unjust action. The specific attention he gave to this condition was immediately prompted by his awareness of the restiveness of the peoples who are presently captive under unjust rule and who are tempted to believe, not without reason, that their rescue will require the use of force. This condition of probable success is not, of course, simply the statesman's classical political calculus of success. It is the moral calculus that is enjoined in the traditional theory of rebellion against tyranny. Furthermore, Pius XII was careful to warn that in applying this moral calculus regard must be had for the tinderbox character of our world in which a spark may set off a conflagration.

A fourth principle of traditional theory is also affirmed by Pius XII, the principle of limitation in the use of force. It may be a matter of some surprise that he gave so little emphasis and development to it, at least in comparison to the preponderant place that the problem seems to have assumed in the minds of other theorists, Catholic and non-Catholic. There is one formal text. After asserting the legitimacy of "modern total warfare," that is, ABC warfare, under the set of stringent conditions already stated, he added:

Even then every effort must be made and every means taken to avoid it, with the aid of international covenants, or to set limits to its use precise enough so that its effects will be confined to the strict exigencies of defense. In any case, when the employment of this means entails such an extension of the evil that it entirely escapes from the control of man, its use ought to be rejected as immoral. Here it is no longer a question of defense against injustice and of the necessary safeguard of legitimate possessions, but of the annihilation, pure and simple, of all human life within its radius of action. This is not permitted on any account.

This is a very general statement indeed. And it takes the issue at its extreme, where it hardly needs statement, since the moral decision cannot fail to be obvious. Who would undertake to defend on any grounds, including military grounds, the annihilation of all human life within the radius of action of an ABC war that "entirely escapes from the control of man?" [7] We have here an affirmation, if you will, of the rights of innocence, of the distinction between combatant and noncombatant. But it is an extremely broad statement.

One finds in the earlier utterances of Pius XII, when he was demonstrating the first thesis in the traditional doctrine of war (that war is an evil, the fruit of sin), much advertence to "massacres of innocent victims," the killing of "infants with their mothers, the ill and infirm and aged," etc. These tragedies stand high on the list of the evils of war. In the text cited there is no explicit return to this principle of the right of innocence when it is formally a question of total nuclear war and the use of nuclear weapons. If there is an anomaly

[7] Around this time (1954) there was a lot of loose and uninformed talk about weapons that really would go beyond human control; there was talk, for instance, of the so-called "cobalt bomb" and its "unlimited" powers of radioactive contamination. It is impossible to know what were the sources of the pope's scientific information. To my knowledge, he never adverts to the qualitative distinction and radical discontinuity between low-kiloton and high-megaton weapons. The former are not necessarily weapons of mass destruction. Even the latter do not "escape from the control of man"; their blast and fire effects, and their atmosphere-contamination effects, have been fairly exactly measured.

here, the reason for it may lie in the fact that the pope was forcing himself to face the desperate case. And in desperate cases, in which conscience is perplexed, the wise moralist is chary of the explicit and the nice, especially when the issue, as here, is one of social and not individual morality. In such cases hardly more than a *Grenzmoral* is to be looked for or counseled. In fact, the whole Catholic doctrine of war is hardly more than a *Grenzmoral*, an effort to establish on a minimal basis of reason a form of human action, the making of war, that remains always fundamentally irrational.[8]

Two further propositions in the general theory must be mentioned. The first concerns the legitimacy of defense preparations on the part of individual states. Their legitimacy is founded on two actual facts of international life. First, at the moment there does not exist what Pius XII constantly looked forward to as the solution of the problem of war, namely, a constituted international authority possessing a monopoly of the use of armed force in international affairs. Second, there does exist the threat of "brutal violence and lack of conscience." In this factual situation, "the right to be in a posture of defense cannot be denied, even today, to any state." Here again the principle is extremely general; it says nothing about the morality of this or that configuration of the defense establishment of a given nation. The statement does not morally validate everything that goes on at Cape Canaveral or at Los Alamos.

Finally, the Pope of Peace disallowed the validity of conscientious objection. The occasion was the controversy on the subject, notably in Germany, where the resonances of a sort of anticipatory *Fronterlebnis* were giving an alarming impulse to pacifist movements. Particularly in question was the deposit of nuclear weapons on German soil as part of the NATO defense establishment. The pope's judgment was premised on the legitimacy of the government, the democratic openness of its decisions, and the extremity of the historical

---

[8] I am not for a moment suggesting, of course, that the principle of the rights of innocent life has become in any sense irrelevant to the contemporary problem of war. Still less am I suggesting that Pius XII modified the traditional doctrine in this respect. I am merely noting what I noted, sc., that this principle receives no sharp emphasis, to say the least, in his doctrine. There may be other reasons for this than the one that I tentatively suggested in the text above.

82

necessity for making such defense preparations as would be adequate in the circumstances. He concluded that such a government is "acting in a manner that is not immoral" and that "a Catholic citizen may not make appeal to his own conscience as ground for refusing to give his services and to fulfill duties fixed by law." This duty of armed service to the state, and this right of the state to arm for self-defense, are, he added, the traditional doctrine of the Church, even in latter days under Leo XIII and Benedict XV, when the problems of armaments and conscription put a pressing issue to the Christian conscience.

The Relevance of the Doctrine

The foregoing may do as a statement, at least in outline, of the traditional doctrine on war in the form and with the modifications given it by the authority of the Church today. It is not particularly difficult to make this sort of statement. The difficulty chiefly begins after the statement has been made. Not that objections are raised, at least not in Catholic circles, against the doctrine itself as stated. What is queried is the usefulness of the doctrine, its relevance to the concrete actualities of our historical moment. I shall conclude with some comments on this issue.

I think that the tendency to query the uses of the Catholic doctrine on war initially rises from the fact that it has for so long not been used, even by Catholics. That is, it has not been made the basis for a sound critique of public policies, and as a means for the formation of a right public opinion. The classic example, of course, was the policy of "unconditional surrender" during the last war. This policy clearly violated the requirement of the "right intention" that has always been a principle in the traditional doctrine of war. Yet no sustained criticism was made of the policy by Catholic spokesmen. Nor was any substantial effort made to clarify by moral judgment the thickening mood of savage violence that made possible the atrocities of Hiroshima and Nagasaki. I think it is true to say that the traditional doctrine was irrelevant during World War II. This is no argument against the traditional doctrine. The Ten Commandments do not lose their imperative relevance by reason of the fact that they are violated. But there is place for an indictment of all of us who failed to make the tradition relevant.

The initial relevance of the traditional doctrine today lies in its value as the solvent of false dilemmas. Our fragmentized culture seems to be the native soil of this fallacious and dangerous type of thinking. There are, first of all, the two extreme positions, a soft sentimental pacifism and a cynical hard realism. Both of these views, which are also "feelings," are formative factors in the moral climate of the moment. Both of them are condemned by the traditional doctrine as false and pernicious. The problem is to refute by argument the false antinomy between war and morality that they assert in common, though in different ways. The further and more difficult problem is to purify the public climate of the miasma that emanates from each of them and tends to smother the public conscience.

A second false dilemma has threatened to dominate the argument on national defense in Germany. It sloganized itself thus: "Lieber rot als tot." It has made the same threat in England, where it has been developed in a symposium by twenty-three distinguished Englishmen entitled, *The Fearful Choice: A Debate on Nuclear Policy.* The choice, of course, is between the desperate alternatives, either universal atomic death or complete surrender to communism. The Catholic mind, schooled in the traditional doctrine of war and peace, rejects the dangerous fallacy involved in this casting up of desperate alternatives. Hidden beneath the fallacy is an abdication of the moral reason and a craven submission to some manner of technological or historical determinism.

It is not, of course, that the traditional doctrine rejects the extreme alternatives as possibilities. Anything in history is possible. Moreover, on grounds of the moral principle of proportion the doctrine supports the grave recommendation of the greatest theorist of war in modern times, von Clausewitz: "We must therefore familiarize ourselves with the thought of an honorable defeat." Conversely, the doctrine condemns the hysteria that swept Washington in August, 1958, when the Senate voted, eighty-two to two, to deny governmental funds to any person or institution who ever proposes or actually conducts any study regarding the "surrender of the government of the U.S." [9] "Losing," said von Clausewitz, "is a function of winning," thus stating in his own military idiom the moral calculus prescribed by traditional moral doctrine. The moralist agrees with the military theorist that the essence of a military situation is uncertainty. And when he requires, with Pius XII, a solid probability of success as a moral ground for a legitimate use of arms, he must reckon with the possibility of failure and be prepared to accept it. But this is a moral decision, worthy of a man and of a civilized nation. It is a free, morally motivated, and responsible act, and therefore it inflicts no stigma of dishonor. It is not that "weary resignation," condemned by Pius XII, which is basic to the inner attitude of the theorists of the desperate alternatives, no matter which one they argue for or accept.

On the contrary, the single inner attitude which is nourished by the traditional doctrine is a will to peace, which, in the extremity, bears

[9] When "Washington" thinks of "surrender," it apparently can think only of "unconditional" surrender. Thus does the demonic specter of the past hover over us, as a still imperious *rector harum tenebrarum*. Thus patriotism, once the last refuge of the scoundrel, now has become the first refuge of the fool. It is folly not to foresee that the United States may be laid in ruins by a nuclear attack; the folly is compounded by a decision not to spend any money on planning what to do after that not-impossible event. There is no room today for the heroic romanticism of the apocryphal utterance, "The Old Guard dies but never surrenders." Even Victor Hugo did not put this line on the lips of Cambronne; he simply had him say, "Merde." For all its vulgarity, this was a far more sensible remark in the circumstances. For my part, I am impressed by the cold rationality of Soviet military thought as described by Raymond L. Garthoff, *Soviet Strategy in the Nuclear Age* (New York, 1958): "The fundamental Soviet objectives which determine political and military strategies may be concisely summarized in one: Advance the power of the Soviet Union in whatever ways are most expedient so long as the survival of the Soviet power itself is not endangered" (p. 5). For the Soviet Union survival is not an issue in war; for us it is the only issue. In Soviet thought military action is subordinate to political aims; with us military action creates its own aims, and there is only one, "victory," sc., unconditional surrender. "The Soviet strategic concept, in the thermonuclear era as before, is founded on the belief that the primary objective of military operations is the destruction of hostile military forces, and not the annihilation of the economic and population resources of the enemy. Thus contemporary American views often diverge sharply from this traditional stand" (pp. 71–72). Finally, Soviet policy envisages the "long war" even after a massive exchange of thermonuclear weapons (pp. 87–91). With us, if deterrence fails, and this massive exchange occurs, that is the end; we have no policy after that, except stubbornly to maintain that it is up to the enemy, and not us, to surrender — unconditionally. There is no little irony in the fact that the communist enemy seems to understand better than we do the traditional doctrine on the uses of force.

85

within itself a will to enforce the precept of peace by arms. But this will to arms is a moral will; for it is identically a will to justice. It is formed under the judgment of reason. And the first alternative contemplated by reason, as it forms the will to justice through the use of force, is not the possibility of surrender, which would mean the victory of injustice. This is the ultimate extremity, beyond even the extremity of war itself. Similarly, the contrary alternative considered by reason is not a general annihilation, even of the enemy. This would be worse than injustice; it would be sheer folly. In a word, a debate on nuclear policy that is guided by the traditional doctrine of war does not move between the desperate alternatives of surrender or annihilation. If it means simply an honorable defeat, surrender may be morally tolerable; but it is not to be tolerated save on a reasonable calculus of proportionate moral costs. In contrast, annihilation is on every count morally intolerable; it is to be averted at all costs, that is, at the cost of every effort, in every field, that the spirit of man can put forth.

Precisely here the proximate and practical value, use, and relevance of the traditional doctrine begin to appear. Its remote value may lie in its service as a standard of casuistry on various kinds of war.[10] Its remote value certainly lies in its power to form the public conscience and to clarify the climate of moral opinion in the midst of today's international conflict. But its proximate value is felt at the crucial point where the moral and political orders meet. Primarily, its value resides in its capacity to set the right terms for rational debate on public policies bearing on the problem of war and peace in this age,[11] characterized by international conflict and by advanced

[10] I use the subjunctive because I do not know how many wars in history would stand up under judgment by the traditional norms, or what difference it made at the time whether they did or not.

[11] I am not sure that one should talk today in these categories, "war and/or peace," leaving unexamined the question just what their validity is as moral and political categories. The basic fallacy is to suppose that "war" and "peace" are two discontinuous and incommensurable worlds of existence and universes of discourse, each with its own autonomous set of rules, "peace" being the world of "morality" and "war" being the world of "evil," in such wise that there is no evil as long as there is peace and no morality as soon as there is war. This is a common American assumption. Moreover, it would help greatly to attend to the point made by Mr. Philip C. Jessup that we live today

technology. This is no mean value, if you consider the damage that is being presently done by argument carried on in the wrong terms.

The traditional doctrine disqualifies as irrelevant and dangerous the false dilemmas of which I have spoken. It also rejects the notion that the big problem is to "abolish war" or "ban the bomb." It is true that the traditional doctrine on war looks forward to its own disappearance as a chapter in Catholic moral theology. The effort of the moral reason to fit the use of violence into the objective order of justice is paradoxical enough; but the paradox is heightened when this effort takes place at the interior of the Christian religion of love. In any case, the principles of the doctrine themselves make clear that our historical moment is not destined to see a moral doctrine of war discarded as unnecessary. War is still the possibility, not to be exorcised even by prayer and fasting. The Church does not look immediately to the abolition of war. Her doctrine still seeks to fulfill its triple traditional function: to condemn war as evil, to limit the evils it entails, and to humanize its conduct as far as possible.

"Limited War"

In the light of the traditional doctrine and in the no less necessary light of the facts of international life and technological development today, what are the right terms for argument on public policy? These are readily reached by a dialectical process, an alternation between principle and fact. The doctrine asserts, in principle, that force is still the *ultima ratio* in human affairs, and that its use in extreme circumstances may be morally obligatory *ad repellendam injuriam*. The facts assert that today this *ultima ratio* takes the form of nuclear force, whose use remains possible and may prove to be necessary, lest a free field be granted to brutal violence and lack of conscience. The doctrine asserts that the use of nuclear force must be limited, the principle of limitation being the exigencies of legitimate defense

in an "intermediate state" between peace and war; he contends that, "if one were accustomed to the idea of intermediacy, it can be argued that the likelihood of 'total war' could be diminished. . . . The basic question is whether our concepts, our terminology, our law have kept pace with the evolution of international affairs" (*American Journal of International Law*, 48 [1954], 98ff.).

against injustice. Thus the terms of public debate are set in two words, "limited war." All other terms of argument are fanciful or fallacious. (I assume here that the argument is to be cast primarily in political terms, only secondarily in military terms; for armed force is never more than a weapon of policy, a weapon of last resort.)

I shall not attempt to construct the debate itself. But two points may be made. First, there are those who say that the limitation of nuclear war, or any war, is today impossible, for a variety of reasons — technical, political, etc. In the face of this position, the traditional doctrine simply asserts again, "The problem today is limited war." But notice that the assertion is on a higher plane than that of sheer fact. It is a moral proposition, or better, a moral imperative. In other words, since nuclear war may be a necessity, it must be made a possibility. Its possibility must be created. And the creation of its possibility requires a work of intelligence, and the development of manifold action, on a whole series of policy levels — political (foreign and domestic), diplomatic, military, technological, scientific, fiscal, etc., with the important inclusion of the levels of public opinion and public education. To say that the possibility of limited war cannot be created by intelligence and energy, under the direction of a moral imperative, is to succumb to some sort of determinism in human affairs.

My second point is that the problem of limited war would seem to require solution in two stages. One stage consists in the construction of a sort of "model" of the limited war. This is largely a problem in conceptual analysis. Its value consists in making clear the requirements of limited war in terms of policy on various levels.[12] Notably it makes clear that a right order must prevail among policies. It makes clear, for instance, that the limitation of war becomes difficult or impossible if fiscal policy assumes the primacy over armament policy,

[12] The most significant attempt in this direction was made by Henry A. Kissinger, *Nuclear Weapons and Foreign Policy* (New York, 1957). The validity of his theories on limited war (chaps. 5–7) has been contested on technical and other grounds. The more permanent value of the book may lie in its convincing argument that a vacuum of doctrine, military as well as moral, lies at the heart of the whole vast defense establishment of the United States (cf. chap. 12 and *passim*).

or if armament policy assumes the primacy over military policy, or if military policy assumes the primacy over foreign policy in the political sense.

The second stage is even more difficult. It centers on a *quaestio facti*. The fact is that the international conflict, in its ideological as in its power dimension, comes to concrete expression in certain localized situations, each of which has its own peculiarities. The question then is, where and under what circumstances is the irruption of violence possible or likely, and how is the limitation of the conflict to be effected in these circumstances, under regard of political intentions, as controlling of military necessities *in situ*. The answer to this question is what is meant by the formulation of policy. Policy is the hand of the practical reason set firmly upon the course of events. Policy is what a nation does in this or that given situation. In the concreteness of policy, therefore, the assertion of the possibility of limited war is finally made, and made good. Policy is the meeting place of the world of power and the world of morality, in which there takes place the concrete reconciliation of the duty of success that rests upon the statesman and the duty of justice that rests upon the civilized nation that he serves.

Toward a Politico-Moral Science

I am thus led to one final comment on the problem of war. It may be that the classical doctrine of war needs more theoretical elaboration in order to relate it more effectively to the unique conflict that agitates the world today, in contrast with the older historical conflicts upon which the traditional doctrine sought to bear, and by which in turn it was shaped.[13] In any case, another work of the reflective in-

---

[13] It may be that Jessup's "basic question" may legitimately be raised in connection with the theory of the just war as fashioned by later scholasticism. There is always room for a respectful inquiry, whether a proposed "doctrine" is really the tradition or only an *opinio recepta*. What troubled Vanderpol now troubles others, sc., the subtle impact on the traditional doctrine exerted by the modern concept of the sovereign national state. It might be argued that the traditional doctrine has not absorbed this impact without damage to itself. (The same argument, incidentally, might be made with regard to the traditional doctrine on Church-State relations.) In this connection cf. J. T. Delos, "A Sociology of Modern War and the Theory of the Just War," *Cross Currents*, 8 (1958), 248–66.

telligence and study is even more badly needed. I shall call it a politico-moral analysis of the divergent and particular conflict-situations that have arisen or are likely to arise in the international scene as problems in themselves and as manifestations of the under-lying crisis of our times. It is in these particular situations that war actually becomes a problem. It is in the midst of their dense material-ity that the *quaestio juris* finally rises. To answer it is the function of the moralist, the professional or the citizen moralist. His answer will never be more than an act of prudence, a practical judgment in-formed by principle. But he can give no answer at all to the *quaestio juris* until the *quaestio facti* has been answered. From the point of view of the problem of war and morality the same need appears that has been descried elsewhere in what concerns the more general prob-lem of politics and morality. I mean the need of a far more vigorous cultivation of politico-moral science, with close attention to the enor-mous impact of technological developments on the moral order as well as on the political order.

The whole concept of force has undergone a rapid and radical transformation, right in the midst of history's most acute political crisis. One consequence of these two related developments was em-phasized by Panel Two, "International Security: The Military As-pect," of the Special Studies Project of the Rockefeller Brothers Fund: "The overall United States strategic concept lags behind de-velopments in technology and in the world political situation." This vacuum of military doctrine greatly troubled the members of the panel. But I know from my own association with the Special Studies Project that they were even more troubled by another vacuum in contemporary thought, sc., the absence of an over-all political-moral doctrine with regard to the uses of force. This higher doctrine is needed to give moral sense and political direction to a master strate-gic concept. "Power without a sense of direction," they said, "may drain life of its meaning, if it does not destroy humanity altogether." This sense of direction cannot be found in technology; of itself, tech-nology tends toward the exploitation of scientific possibilities simply because they are possibilities. Power can be invested with a sense of direction only by moral principles. It is the function of morality

90

to command the use of power, to forbid it, to limit it; or, more in general, to define the ends for which power may or must be used and to judge the circumstances of its use. But moral principles cannot effectively impart this sense of direction to power until they have first, as it were, passed through the order of politics; that is, until they have first become incarnate in public policy. It is public policy in all its varied concretions that must be "moralized" (to use an abused word in its good sense). This is the primary need of the moment. For my part, I am not confident that it is being met.

chapter VI

Morality of Nuclear Armament

by John R. Connery, S.J.

THE TRULY Christian conscience with its sincere regard for the
dignity of the human person is shocked at any violence directed
against human beings. Even when associated with legitimate self-
defense, the need for violence evokes feelings of deep regret, especially when it results in the loss of human life. This is as it should
be. A moral conscience sensitive to violence is our best safeguard
against any excess in this direction.

But regret over the need for violence in repelling unjust aggression
is in itself no reflection on the morality of the defense itself. However
distasteful, the use of violence may be perfectly legitimate, and although the regret and distaste may increase with the degree of violence demanded by the situation, neither the intensity of the distress
nor the measure of the violence resorted to can be used as independ-
ent moral yardsticks. The morality of the violence will depend on its
proportion to the aggression. One will not rout a burglar with an
atomic bomb. The moral conscience will allow for adequate defense,
but it will not tolerate unnecessary or disproportionate violence.

When the aggression is on an individual level, the moral problem of defense may be simple enough. It is relatively easy to accommodate defense measures to an individual act of aggression. But when the aggression takes place on a national level, the problem of defense assumes a much more complex character. The concept of "total war" has been advanced in recent times, but moralists are still generally agreed that, although more people are actually involved in warfare today than in former times, a distinction between combatant and noncombatant must still prevail. This distinction makes defense against an aggressor nation a much more delicate problem than defense against an individual aggressor. How can one defend oneself adequately against an aggressor nation and still maintain a distinction between combatant and noncombatant?

It is in this connection that the quantitative aspect of defense measures takes on a greater moral significance. And it is precisely in this area that nuclear warfare creates a serious moral problem. The greater the destructive potential of the weapon, the less discriminating is the warfare likely to be. It would seem that present nuclear weapons, such as the H-bomb, either have been, or at least can be, developed far beyond the demands of any single known military target. The use of such weapons, then, carries with it the necessary destruction of noncombatants or at least nonmilitary objects.

It is with these large-sized nuclear weapons that we are concerned. Must there be some limit to the size and the number of such weapons in our armament program? That such limitation is a desirable goal for world peace conferences no one will deny. But it is difficult to say whether even limited disarmament on a world-wide scale can be hoped for in the present world situation. Even if agreements could be arrived at, it is not clear just how reliable they would be. For practical purposes, then, it is necessary to consider the prospect of limitation of nuclear weapons on a unilateral basis. Would such a unilateral limitation of armaments be dictated by moral considerations of an imperative nature? Or to put the question more concretely: Is the use of destructive weapons of megatonic or multi-megatonic proportions an absolutely unjustifiable war measure?

Indiscriminate Warfare

Given an isolated military target of such proportions that nuclear destructive forces would be required to eliminate it effectively, all moralists would agree that the use of such weapons would be justified. But this would seem to be a purely theoretical case, hardly realized in modern warfare. The actual situation in the modern world is that the war potential of nations is concentrated in heavily populated areas. The use of megatonic destructive forces on such targets would necessarily carry with it tremendous civilian losses. Would this necessarily be classified as indiscriminate warfare?

Moralists agree that the noncombatant may not be the direct target of any destructive weapon, large or small. This means that one may neither deliberately aim his attack at noncombatants nor drop bombs without distinction on combatants and noncombatants alike. Such bombing would be contrary to sound moral principles, even if resorted to only in retaliation.

It would be equally immoral to direct even at a military target a weapon whose destructive power would go far beyond the demands of the defense, especially if it were uncontrollable. Such an attack could hardly be interpreted as other than indiscriminate and irresponsible warfare.

But granted a sufficiently important military target which could not be safely eliminated by any less drastic means, nuclear bombing would be morally justified, even if it involved the resultant loss of a large segment of the civilian population. It is presumed, of course, that the good to be achieved is at least equal to the expected damages.

Perennial Problem

The unavoidable loss of civilian life consequent upon a legitimate attack on a military target is not a moral problem peculiar to nuclear warfare. It has always been a problem of warfare. And moralists have always recognized that this indirect loss of civilian life was allowable, if the alternative was an equivalent loss to the defender. But there is a vast difference from the moral standpoint between attacking noncombatants and allowing their death incident to a legitimate attack on combatants. The latter is an unwanted and un-avoidable adjunct to a legitimate moral defense.

But to be justified, the loss of civilian life must be unavoidable and balanced by a proportionate good to the defender. Thus, if precision bombing of individual industrial plants in enemy territory would achieve the same result with less loss of civilian life than nuclear bombing of a whole industrial area, the latter would not be justified. But if precision bombing would mean losses to the defender equivalent to the civilian losses resulting to the enemy from nuclear bombing, the latter could legitimately be employed.

To illustrate, let us suppose that in a city in enemy territory there are two war plants which I want to eliminate. They are in the same area of that city but separated by a small residential section. I can knock out these plants by precision bombing; or I can knock them out by one superbomb, but with concomitant destruction of the civilian area between them. If I can achieve my goal with precision bombing of the individual plants, I would not be allowed to bomb the whole industrial area. But if precision bombing would be very costly to me both in money and in the lives of my own men, so that I could honestly say that my losses in such bombing would be proportionate to the loss of civilian life in bombing the industrial area, the use of the superbomb would be morally justified.

Now, whether the case concerns two industrial plants in the same area, or two industrial areas in the same city, or even two industrial cities in the same region, though the application is more appalling, the principle remains the same.

Sufficient Reason

An important consideration, of course, in deciding between precision bombing and large-scale bombing of an industrial area is the military strength of the enemy. Thus, for instance, if my enemy were in possession of nuclear bombs which I had good reason to believe he would use, it would be suicidal for me to choose the more leisurely precision bombing. His possession of such weapons would never justify a direct attack on his civilian population but it would give me the sufficient reason to knock out his war potential as quickly and as effectively as possible, even with a tremendous loss of civilian life. The only alternative to a quick and fatal blow at his war machine would be the destruction of my own population — which is certainly a sufficient reason for allowing the incidental, though perhaps staggering, losses to the enemy.

These are awe-inspiring, and even terrifying, reflections. They point up the critical need of effective agreements among nations to limit armaments. But they also bring out, I believe, the fact that in the absence of such agreements moral considerations will not force conscientious nations into a position of military inferiority.

The Moralist's Role

A moralist does not feel qualified as a moralist to pass judgment on the adequacy of our present nuclear weapons to deal with the modern unjust aggressor. He can only set up the moral framework for the licit use of such weapons. It is up to the scientist and the military expert to decide when the weapons we have at our disposal are adequate to a defense within that framework. Certainly, if we have at our disposal nuclear weapons adequate to a legitimate defense against any foreseeable aggression, one could hardly justify the production of more destructive weapons. The possession of such weapons would be tantamount to an invitation to unnecessary and irresponsible destruction. Moreover, if present nuclear weapons carry with them large-scale civilian losses and damage, moral considerations would demand that some effort be made to eliminate the destruction not essential to the military effort. And if, for instance, some bomb could be developed with all the explosive power of the H-bomb but without the subsequent contamination of civilian areas, the use of the H-bomb could hardly be justified. But any other move in the direction of unilateral limitation of armaments or even disarmament would be on a voluntary rather than an obligatory basis.

Whether a voluntary move toward unilateral disarmament would ease the world situation without at the same time weakening our own position is matter for a prudential decision on the part of those who are in possession of all the facts of the case. It may be that in a situation where agreements among nations cannot be reached or trusted the best guarantee against the use of the bomb will be the fact that both parties are in possession of it. In support of this position one might advance the experience with mustard gas during World War II. A somewhat embarrassing examination of conscience regarding the use of the A-bomb at Hiroshima and Nagasaki might lead to the same conclusion. Would we have used the bomb if we were not sure that the enemy was in no position to retaliate in kind? These experiences are not in themselves decisive but they should certainly be taken into consideration in any decision relating to unilateral disarmament.

chapter VII

The Hydrogen Bombing of Cities

by John C. Ford, S.J.

INSTEAD OF thinking of Moscow as the target of an all-out multi-megaton H-bomb attack, let us imagine a more familiar scene: the New York-Newark area, with its ten million inhabitants and important military targets. Would it be permissible, in order to win a just war, to wipe out such an area with death or grave injury, resulting indiscriminately, to the majority of its ten million inhabitants?

In my opinion the answer must be in the negative. If I assert that it is wrong to kill a million schoolchildren, I do not have to prove my assertion. It is those who assert the contrary who have the burden of the proof.

Catholic teaching has been unanimous for long centuries in declaring that it is never permitted to kill directly noncombatants in wartime. Why? Because they are innocent. That is, they are innocent of the violent and destructive action of war, or of any close participation in the violent and destructive action of war. It is such participation *alone* that would make them legitimate targets of violent repression themselves.

98

Total War

It is the fashion to say: "But today war is different. War is total. Everybody, or almost everybody, in the enemy country contributes to the war effort. Everybody is more or less a combatant." This is fallacious.

It is true that the wearing of a uniform is no longer the criterion of combatant status. It is true that to a great extent civilian participation has increased. But even if it were ten times what it used to be, that increase is comparatively insignificant. The real, significant difference between war three hundred years ago and war today is that man has increased his destructive attacking power not ten but ten thousand times, and has learned to carry that destructive power hundreds of times faster to the very heart of every civilian population on earth. Air power and nuclear weapons have done it.

That is the only true sense in which modern war is total. It is total because the total civilian population can be subjected to total violent attack and totally annihilated by it. Modern war is not total in the sense that all the civilians, or almost all of them, or anywhere near the majority of them, are waging it, that is, prosecuting it by violent action, or by cooperating closely in its violent prosecution. Contributing to the war effort does not make a person a combatant. A ten-year-old girl saves bottle caps for the scrap steel drive. She contributes to the war effort. In fact, she helps to make munitions. May I shoot her down on the theory that she is a combatant, an unjust aggressor, and therefore a legitimate target for total violent repression? No Catholic theologian would ever assert such a thing.

The New York-Newark area is one of the most highly industrialized areas on earth. But, stretching the term "combatant" to the very limit and beyond all reasonable limits, and including in it all the employees of all manufacturing industries of every kind, and all those engaged in public utilities, in transportation, in communications, and in contract construction in that whole area (in 1951), they would all together constitute less than 25 per cent of the total ten million inhabitants. Three-quarters of that population, seven and one-half million people, are innocent human beings, innocent of the one thing which in our theology would make them legitimate targets of direct violence, namely violent war-making, or sufficiently close cooperation in violent war-making.

Direct Intention

But it may be urged that the hydrogen bombing of cities could be justified because there would be no *direct* intention of killing the innocent — that the death or maiming of millions of innocent people would not be intentional. It would merely be the reluctantly permitted side effect of a good action, the destruction of military targets. It is my contention that the civil and military leaders who would plan and execute the dropping of a series of high megaton H-bombs on an area like Moscow or New York: 1) *would not* in practice avoid the direct intention of violence to the innocent; *2) could not* avoid such an intention even if they would; and *3)* even if they would and could avoid it, would have no *proportionate justifying* reason for permitting the evils which this type of all-out nuclear warfare would let loose.

In the first place it is unreal to imagine that policy makers and military leaders will restrict their intention to the destruction of military targets and combatant personnel. In the last war when we really wanted to hit only military targets, as in the bombing of Rome, we made sure that was all we hit. When we wanted to "destroy enemy morale" we bombed out whole areas of densely populated cities. The *United States Strategic Bomber Survey* declared that area bombing was "intended primarily to destroy morale, particularly that of the industrial worker." An official Army Air Force publication, *Target: Germany*, made it clear that the purpose of the bombing was "terror and devastation carried to the core of the warring nation." Terror bombing means killing and maiming innocent noncombatants in order to frighten the resistance out of those who survive. We did this in Germany. If we do not intend to do it again, why are we stockpiling large quantities of high-megaton H-bombs? The military targets for such bombs are few and far between. If we are really intending to hit only military targets, why do we not concentrate on the smaller nuclear weapons which can be honestly aimed at military objectives? It is academic and unreal to talk about the principle of the double effect where it is clear that the actual intent will be to win the war by wiping out everything in sight.

In the second place, they could not avoid the direct intent even if they would. If I saw a black widow spider crawling across the shiny bald pate of my neighbor, could I take a sledge hammer and swing it down full on the spider, intending directly only the death of the spider? Could I honestly say I had no direct intention of killing the man? Especially if there were a flyswatter handy? Notice the question is not whether it would be permissible to act this way. No one would permit it. The question is whether it is psychologically and honestly possible to avoid the direct intent of killing which seems to be implicit in my choice of the sledge hammer in those circumstances.

Incidental Effect

There comes a point where the immediate evil effect of a given action is so overwhelmingly large in its physical extent, in its mere bulk, by comparison with the immediate good effect, that it no longer makes sense to say that it is merely incidental, not directly intended, but reluctantly permitted. It is not a question of the physical inevitability of the evil effect. It is a question of its incidentality. I can see how a bombardier could drop a hydrogen bomb on an enemy fleet at sea, intending directly only the destruction of the fleet, while permitting reluctantly the inevitable deaths of some innocent women and children by chance aboard. But I doubt that the man with the sledge-hammer can intend to kill only the poisonous spider and call the death of his neighbor merely incidental. And I doubt that the air-strategist can drop his H-bombs on New York-Newark and call the resultant deaths of millions of innocent people merely incidental.

Given the size and power of the destructive weapon chosen, given the size and character of the area aimed at, and given the immense extent of the human carnage involved, it does not seem possible any longer to say: "I am making an attack on certain precise and quite limited military targets; all the rest I reluctantly permit as incidental

101

to this military attack." Especially when I have at hand smaller weapons capable of destroying these precise military targets without the mass human carnage.

To my mind common sense repudiates this interpretation of what is happening. Common sense indicates rather that the destruction of the targets is incidental to the destruction of the area; that in choosing the H-bomb as my weapon in these circumstances I am choosing the death of the innocent millions. Merely telling myself that I do not intend this directly will not change the actual state of affiars. I can no longer believe myself.

Proportionate Reason

In the third place, even if the policy makers and military leaders would and could avoid the direct intention of killing millions of innocent people, there cannot be any proportionate reason to justify the evils which this type of all-out nuclear warfare would let loose on the world.

It is illegitimate to appeal to the principle of the double effect when the alleged justifying cause is speculative, future, and problematical, while the evil effect is definite, enormous, certain, and immediate. The hoped-for good effect, in the H-bombing of Moscow, for instance, would presumably be self-preservation from Russia's physical attack and the preservation of our country from the threat of materialistic socialism. But would it work? We do not know. Physically the attack might boomerang. As for the atheistic communism, the extermination of Moscow and the Muscovites might or might not preserve us from it. Ideas have a way of surviving bombardments, but the millions of innocent do not survive. Their wholesale slaughter is immediate, certain, irrevocable.

Furthermore, if this kind of warfare were once conceded by moralists to be legitimate, it would mean the practical abandonment of any distinction between innocent noncombatants and guilty aggressors — that fundamental distinction which the Catholic Church has taught for centuries. The gains made by Christianity down through the centuries in suppressing the barbarities of war would be lost. We would be adopting, in practice at least, the immorality of total war.

Survival of the Race

Worst of all, it seems entirely probable that once a world-wide war got started, once the high-megaton H-bombs began to fall across the world, there would be at stake, not the survival of this nation or that, but the survival of civilization and even of the human race itself. Einstein said he did not know what weapons would be used in the next war, but in the war after that it would be stone clubs. To H-bomb Moscow would be to embrace the serious risk of such an all-out nuclear war. The probable outcome for the human race? Extinction. No proportionate reason can be assigned for "permitting" the extinction of the human race.

The threat of atheistic communism presents us with terrifying problems. But I think these problems are entirely oversimplified when reduced to the stark dilemma: either wipe them out or be wiped out yourselves. But if that were the dilemma, I would consider that we had arrived at the point where absolute moral imperatives were at stake, and the followers of Christ should abandon themselves totally to divine Providence rather than forsake these imperatives.

chapter VIII

Social Science and the Theology of War

by Gordon C. Zahn

A VERY good friend of mine is forever chiding me for devoting most of my sociological research and writings to issues related to the social problem of war. Why, he asks, do I not put my energy and talents to better use, such as discovering causes and solutions for juvenile delinquency or some equally "practical" contributions? Since this man is an intelligent, well-educated and devout Catholic, a figure of influence in his community, his protests have a rather direct bearing upon the topic to which this volume addresses itself.

The "state of the question" regarding the morality of nuclear war may be simply stated: For all too many Catholics there is no question or, at least, none that falls within the average layman's scope of competence. That this is so may be traced in part to the fact that we have not recognized that the morality of modern war, including *pre-nuclear* war, can or should be a legitimate subject for serious disputation. In this, American Catholics lag far behind their European brethren who have been involved in a serious debate for quite some time. Psychologically the lag may be nothing more than a reflection

104

of a state of self-righteous contentment with the institution of war. After all, ours is a national history of consistent military success. Whatever the cause, however, he who would stir the placid waters by suggesting that there is a question that invites (if it does not demand!) careful consideration and thorough discussion is likely to be told that "these are matters for the theological experts to decide." And if he persists, he will risk the annoyance and displeasure of his hearers and, quite possibly, their suspicious appraisal as a "troublemaker" seeking to "embarrass the Church." My friend represents a reaction somewhere between the two. Pressed, he will grant the legitimacy of the question; yet, he will dismiss its discussion as impractical, a waste of time and effort that might better be spent in attacking some social problem more amenable to solution.

Other friends with whom I have argued the morality of modern war are more inclined to evade the question altogether than to deny its existence. What purpose is served, they ask, by raising an issue which can only lead to conclusions that place impossible burdens upon the individual conscience? The objection can be countered easily enough, but the frame of mind it reveals presents greater difficulty. This tendency to shy away from uncomfortable moral responsibilities, blinding one's eyes and stopping one's ears if need be, bore bitter harvest in the ghastly scandal of World War II. From it stemmed the willingness of German Catholics to resign themselves to active and unquestioning service in the Nazi armies. And this was matched on the Allied side by the moral default of Catholics who collaborated without compunction in the unprecedented slaughter of noncombatant civilians to gain the morally questionable objective of "unconditional surrender." One would have to forgive the pagan observer who, viewing all this, might conclude: Behold these Christians, see how they hate one another!

The atrocities of Hiroshima and Nagasaki served a double function. They put the finishing touches to the world-wide carnival of death and destruction, and, at the same time, they set the stage for future holocausts of unimaginable proportions. In his article Father Ford makes it quite clear that nuclear war brings us face-to-face with what could prove to be the ultimate moral problem, self-destruction of the human race. In a very real sense, this is our special problem as Americans, and it is an extremely urgent one. It was this nation and its totally mobilized material and intellectual resources that produced the murderous weapon. The distinction of being the first and only nation to use it against a human population is also ours. Other nations have since developed nuclear war potential and others will do so in the near future, but the crucial moral problem remains ours to solve. By leading in the development and use of this new means of total destruction, we earned the responsibility to lead the world to a moral judgment of our creation and to the renunciation, even the unilateral renunciation if need be, of its further manufacture and use.

But the nation's responsibility will not be met unless, and until, it faces moral facts and their implications honestly and fearlessly. There is little reason to believe that it is ready to do so. The issue can be stated bluntly: The responsible leaders of our nation are publicly committed to a nuclear war policy that is *at the very least* of extremely doubtful morality and, more than likely, absolutely immoral. To the extent that we, as citizens of a democratic political order, bear responsibility (both direct and indirect!) for the selection of these leaders, some measure of the moral guilt must rest with us. At the moment the immorality of this policy is one of manifest intention, but given the unhappy occasion of international conflict, the immorality would quickly become one of act. Despite this, the Catholic voices we would expect to find raised in protest against such a policy are either complacently silent or, as is often the case, raised in its defense. This, unfortunately, is the "state of the question."

Let me be more specific. Official national spokesmen have been quite emphatic in proclaiming the policy of "massive retaliation" or its variously expressed equivalents. Record defense budgets give open evidence of enormous expenditures devoted to the development of nuclear weapons and the means of delivering them. The nation is bound by international commitments that are quite specific; the statements of Lord Montgomery and Secretary Wilson, quoted by Colonel Moriarty, are relevant here. More recent and even more emphatic is General Norstad's 1958 declaration to the Western European Union: "There must be absolutely no misunderstanding about the determination of this alliance to use nuclear weapons in case of aggression." The principal locus of the determination and the prospective source of the weapons are perfectly obvious.

These frank declarations of intention are paralleled by official reports describing some of the weapons that will be involved, and one must assume that the workings of security are such that the more advanced accomplishments in weaponry are still wrapped in military secrecy. What we do know, however, is more than sufficient to serve as a basis for critical moral judgment. For instance, press reports of the successful 1958 test shot of the Atlas missile told of the official jubilation over its "remarkable accuracy." As the *Chicago Sun-Times* explained, "The Air Force missile landed within 30 miles of target. . . . Accuracy within 50 miles is considered sufficient with a nuclear warhead." Although some may be willing to accept this highly flexible definition of the concept, I am rash enough to insist that "accuracy within 50 miles" is no accuracy at all! Certainly this great a margin of error built into the destructive range of a weapon should automatically exclude it from all consideration as a "just means" of warfare.

More recent statements, including the 1960 State of the Union message, claim greater accuracy, usually the one- to two-mile radius mentioned by Colonel Moriarty in his paper. But, as he says, "The exact truth of these claims does not matter." The horror lies, not in the margin of error in aim but, rather, in the range of effectiveness that makes such margin of error inconsequential.

Expert scientific testimony generally sets the maximum range of total and near-total blast and fire destruction of multimegaton bombs at "only" five to ten miles. It would seem, then, that the 1958 news report implied a strategy decision which would involve firing clusters of these missiles at target objectives to assure a 50-mile radius of destructiveness and give the 30-mile miss its "remarkable accuracy." If this interpretation is valid, it, in turn, would imply a policy decision to restrict the use of these weapons to objectives warranting such expensive strategic bombings. Such objectives would almost certainly have to be the major urban centers of the enemy nation with their predominantly noncombatant civilian populations. Here again we return to Colonel Moriarty's "elementary computations" leading to scores of millions of noncombatant deaths and the probable destruction of civilization itself. The incalculable somatic and genetic effects of the radiation resulting from such an attack may be by-passed in this discussion since they would merely add to an already demonstrable conclusion.

This is no hypothetical case drawn from a moral-guidance handbook. This problem is a matter of public record. It is, therefore, imperative that our moralists come to terms with that problem, that for them, too, there may be "absolutely no misunderstanding about the determination" of national leaders. These moralists can no longer indulge in the luxury of esoteric discussions of hypothetical battleships sailing the high seas, discussions which have thus far protected nuclear warfare from theological condemnation. Megaton-sized bombs and the missiles which will deliver them are being built not for battleships but for cities. Our Catholic spiritual leaders would seem to have a clear obligation to condemn any and all weapons which are suited only to uses which are unquestionably immoral and to inform the faithful that any war involving or anticipating recourse to such unjust means would automatically be an unjust war.

That should not be too much to ask, and yet. . . .

Recently, a relatively minor portion of an advisory report to the president gave favorable attention to artificial birth control as a solution to overpopulation problems in certain areas of the world. Almost immediately it was met by an official denunciation on the part of the American Catholic hierarchy. But when the national government boasts of the successful firing of a weapon designed to slaughter millions of noncombatants and continually reaffirms its readiness to use this weapon in the case of war, *not a single bishop* voices public protest or indignation.

This, too, is a clue to the "state of the question."

All of the foregoing is but an introduction to the thesis proposed by this paper : the single overriding need today is for a truly *relevant* moral theology to replace the sterile formulas and distinctions which have become virtually meaningless in the present world context. This is *not* an appeal for a "revision" of basic moral truths. Quite the contrary. We must insist that the principles of the natural law and the Christian revelation cannot change. It is their very immutability that makes it all the more essential that these principles be continually reinterpreted and reapplied to an ever-changing social reality.

Theology and social science come together at this point. True, it is not always recognized that the latter has a valid contribution to make. A personal experience may illustrate this. Drawing upon the results of my research in Germany, I composed an article dealing with the social force of nationalism and its distorting effect upon moral judgments. The editor of a leading Catholic scholarly journal considered it for publication but finally decided that the issue was so complex that it had to be treated from the theological and not the sociological point of view. Perhaps it is the wounded pride of the rejected author speaking, but I feel the editor was wrong. His decision would seem to erect a "wall of separation" between the two disciplines that would make it most difficult, if not impossible, for moral theology to achieve the contemporaneity and relevance it so sorely needs.

This jealous concern for boundaries is not a new issue for the sociologist. Usually, however, he encounters it in the warnings of his colleagues who fear the slightest intrusion of moral considerations will destroy all prospects of scientific objectivity. I have always rejected the sterile superficiality of such exaggerated positivism. Just as enthusiastically do I reject the notion that the theologian holds exclusive domain over all reference to the moral dimensions of observable social behavior. There is an area of overlap here in which each discipline can and should serve the other. Unfortunately, this ideal relationship has yet to be attained, and both have suffered as a result. Social science has shut itself off from many valuable insights and theoretical frameworks in its blind commitment to the myth of the "value-free science." But the loss to moral theology is even more serious in that it has missed the opportunity to take into account the sociological organization and analysis of social facts that could provide it with the full empirical dimensions of responsible human behavior. The sociologist's loss is reflected in incomplete or otherwise

109

inadequate descriptions and analyses; but the moralist's is ultimately measured in terms of at least materially sinful behavior on the part of those who are denied the moral guidance and clarification that might otherwise have been theirs.

This applies with brutal directness to the theological approach to modern war and, most particularly, nuclear war. I submit that the majority of Catholic moralists have either ignored or avoided this crucial moral problem; or, if they have dealt with it, produced interpretations and conclusions almost totally irrelevant to the actual phenomenon of modern war and the policies and behavior it demands.

Admittedly, it is not the sociologist's function to resolve theological problems; but he is certainly competent to state the problem and to evaluate the adequacy (in a behavioral sense) of the solutions offered by the moralist. This is the limited objective set for the present paper. A note of caution should be added, however. I write not only as a sociologist but also as a Catholic who Father Murray would probably classify as a "relative" pacifist with some tendency toward "absolute pacifism." I suspect this is one of the principal reasons for my being invited to contribute to this volume. Nevertheless, while I frankly admit to a point of view, this is not an essay designed primarily to convert the reader to pacifism. Instead, it will seek to outline some areas of special concern and raise questions which, I confidently believe, will ultimately lead the moralist to answers and solutions establishing the validity of the pacifist position. Since this is a limited objective, the reader is advised not to regard this essentially peripheral treatment as a comprehensive or systematic presentation of the pacifist implications of Christianity.

To proceed, then, I contend that our present theology of war is seriously lacking in relevance. Further, I would explain this in terms of four specific reasons or failings: First, it relies on abstract categories and distinctions that are no longer applicable to the kind of war Christians are called upon to wage. Second, it holds to utterly anachronistic formulations of Caesar-God and citizen-ruler relationships, rights and responsibilities. Third, it avoids or mitigates the actual application of moral principles to on-going or impending wars out of a rigid devotion to a distorted image of the virtue of prudence.

And, finally, as a result of these failings, it finds itself unprepared to meet its obligation to alert the individual Christian to his true responsibilities and to assist him in readying himself for the difficult decisions and sacrifices he may be called upon to make.

Let us take, for example, the overly facile applications of the "principle of the double effect," a "principle" which is fast becoming a moral slide rule by which almost any act of war can be justified. These applications begin with the extremely unrealistic assumption that military planners (or the individuals assigned specific tasks) carefully weigh the morally "good effect" against the "evil" and act only when the former is preponderant ("willing only the good," of course). This is utter nonsense. Military planners operate on the basis of military expediency, and individual soldiers are trained to operate on the basis of unquestioning obedience to their military superiors. If any "evil effect" does enter the strategic calculations, it will consist of such things as expenditure of one's own men and materiel, the possible strengthening of enemy resistance, the danger of enemy reprisal, etc. Moral considerations, if they carry any weight at all, will be set in terms of estimated reaction on the part of world opinion; needless to add, in cases of military extremity, their weight would never be decisive. Hiroshima and the decisions of the Nazi high command are cases in point.

Not only is it nonsense to assume that it is being done; but it reveals a hopeless ignorance of human psychology to assume that such a "weighing" would (or *could*) be accomplished in an aura of pure objectivity. Men in crisis-situations simply do not act in a state of emotional detachment. Nationalistic prides and sentiments (both of which are intentionally cultivated and manipulated through organized propaganda efforts), to say nothing of war-induced hatreds and fears, necessarily enter into the behavioral equation and usually are sufficient to tip the balance. Theological determinations of the "principle of the double effect" which ignore this fact are truly psychological absurdities. The lure of the lesser evil lies precisely in the fact that the evil we "must" do is always less than the evil we might otherwise have to endure. In the realm of copybook distinctions it may be a simple matter to divide the bombing of a city into separate acts of willed destruction of a war production plant and unwilled (though fully known and foreseen!) destruction of thousands of innocent noncombatants. But it demands too much to believe that the man who loosed the bomb availed himself of such convenient moral schizophrenia — or that he saw any need for doing so. Our intensive military training programs are designed to free men from the necessity of making such calculations by establishing in them as nearly automatic systems of stimulus-response patterns as possible. As far as the victims of his act are concerned, our bomber friend had been rigorously trained to think of them either as purely expendable units or in terms of hatred- or fear-inducing stereotypes which make those victims fully deserving of their fate.

The military training program is crucial to the argument in that it may be seen as a set of social controls designed to subject the individual trainee to a process of systematic depersonalization in the interest of increased military efficiency. The self-image of the morally responsible person vanishes and is replaced by a new orientation in which the individual sees himself as an agent of destructive force completely responsive to the decisions and directives of his military superiors. This new "self-image" — and the awareness that his enemy counterpart has undergone the same change — makes it possible for him to assume the role of professional killer and to perform acts which, under other circumstances, he would have found unthinkable.

How else could he bridge the gap between the friendly repairman and the soldier spraying fiery death upon his screaming victims, between the playful collegian and the aviator lowering a blanket of death upon a flare-rimmed city? Certainly not by coldly rational calculations of good and evil effects! The secret lies in *conditioning* and not in conviction. The depersonalized agent sees no alternative; like Pilate, he washes his hands of all responsibility, leaving that to those who made the decisions and issued the orders. It also helps if he can be conditioned to regard the objects of his kill as similarly depersonalized agents — as the abstraction he knows simply as "enemy," — not as men with bodies that bleed and burn, with families and friends to mourn them, with loves and hopes and fears like his own. Once this level of conditioning is achieved, all things are possible. Men will follow orders to "take no prisoners"; or, having already taken them, to "deliver them to Paris, and be back in ten minutes." It becomes possible for them to liquidate innocent hostages in reprisal for a guerrilla raid without suffering too many troubling qualms of conscience. *In a very real sense, atrocities are the hallmark of the perfectly accomplished military training program; for they represent the ultimate of obedience to military discipline.*

Fortunately, the "ideal" is rarely achieved despite the total mobilization of psychological talent and resources. But it is achieved often enough — or, even when the finished product falls short of that ideal, the partial success is sufficient — to justify firm theological condemnation of that violation of God's proudest creation which depersonalization and dehumanization represents.

A very specific example, which again is in no sense hypothetical, may be in order here. A few years ago, a network radio program devoted a Sunday to "on the scene" interviews at one of the nation's basic training centers. One such interview featured the instructor charged with the task of training the young recruits in the use of the bayonet. He complained that he encountered a great deal of resistance from the trainees who were naturally repelled by the idea of plunging this weapon into the vitals of a living human being. But he had solved his pedagogical problem in a rather ingenious fashion. Experience had shown that this initial resistance faded away if the men were induced to imitate the roars and snarls of wild beasts as they charged the training dummy. To conclude the interview, a microphone was attached to the dummy so that the listening public might be entertained by the sounds of the recruits as they growled and ripped away at their mock victim.

This, one assumes, is the much-praised "making of men" that only recently was recommended by one of our leading bishops as the solution to the problem of juvenile delinquency. Perhaps this is a special case, and the use of this technique is not widespread. But, widespread or not, this "making of men into beasts" is thoroughly in keeping with the demands of modern war.

The advent of nuclear war aggravates but does not essentially

113

change the situation discussed here. Of course, it may no longer be necessary for the button-pushing killer of future wars to snarl like a tiger; but some other devices will have to be found to free him from his "squeamish" human tendency to view his acts in terms of their consequences and his moral responsibility for those consequences. The bayonet can claim but one victim at a time; the flame-thrower counts its score by the tens; and hundreds, perhaps thousands, will die from the cruel shower of "conventional" bombs; but the button-pusher will have to find some way of adjusting to the ghastly fact that he counts his "kill" in terms of hundreds of thousands or even millions.

A relevant moral theology would have to address itself to this man's moral problem. Unfortunately, our popular moral-guidance handbooks are so filled with discussions of the militant virtues, the "head start to heaven" earned by a battlefield death, and the exhortations to hear the voice of God in the gruff tones of the blustering sergeant that there is little space left for the ugliness of the actual killing. (Sometimes, if one listens carefully, he can almost hear the clank of armor as the valiant knight urges his noble charger on to the fray.)

The lack of relevance of contemporary theology may be traced to the moralist's inability and unwillingness to depart from his copybook abstractions and hairline distinctions. The *inability* arises from the second failing cited earlier, an anachronistic formulation of the Caesar-God and citizen-ruler relationships; the *unwillingness*, from the unfortunate reliance upon an exaggerated notion of "prudence" which all but banishes fortitude from the list of cardinal virtues. Both failings can be clearly illustrated by the records of Catholics and their spiritual leaders in recent wars; both, sad to say, would most likely be just as evident in the event of a future war — that is, unless a whole new emphasis is developed and applied.

Well, not really *new*. What is really called for is a return to an earlier emphasis, the original emphasis which found the Christian ready to follow the Master's advice to give Caesar his due but, at the same time, required that he first make sure that what was demanded of him was really Caesar's due. The historian could fix the exact point of time at which the great change took place when Christianity abandoned its posture of cautious restraint and suspicion toward the state and its demands and started along the path that has led to our present situation in which Caesar's orders are considered binding upon the Christian unless they are demonstrably contrary to the laws of God. The sociologist would be satisfied with saying that the values changed at the time of the conversion of the Empire and that the new value orientation was confirmed and formalized through the rise of scholasticism.

There were good and valid sociological reasons for such a change to take place. All human institutions (and the Church is a human institution in its empirical manifestations) must change as the dynamic ordering of society changes. The direction, form and extent of change will differ for each institution and each new realignment of the total social complex. However, since the Church in its supernatural and nonempirical essence is changeless, its adjustments will not be the product of indifferent evolution or historical accident; on the contrary, each particular change will reflect her judgment of the secular aspects of the new social complex. Thus, in a world dominated by a succession of pagan tyrants bent upon the eradication of the infant Church, one would expect the Church to regard each demand of the secular ruler with a mixture of suspicion and fear; in the post-Constantine world, such suspicion and fear would diminish as confidence grew that the "Christian prince" would use his secular power for the greater honor and glory of God.

There is no need to argue here whether the confidence was deserved or the change wise. It is enough that we waken to the fact that the total social complex has long since changed again and that the time is no longer suited to a theological orientation that may have suited the so-called "Ages of Faith" and the Holy Roman Empire. Whether or not it was wise to replace the original suspicion with a positive attachment to the secular authority, or whether or not the "Christian prince" ever did have real existence outside of theological exercises, are not the points; it is quite certain that neither is applicable today. The sweeping rise of an aggressively jealous nationalism; the advent of liberalism in philosophical, economic and political

115

spheres; the tragic shattering of Christian religious unity; and the concurrent victory of rationalism and scientism in the realm of the intellect — all of these have combined to create a new and essentially un-Christian, even anti-Christian, social complex. *There is no longer any justifiable basis for assuming that the demands of the secular ruler or his intentions will meet even the minimal standards of Christian morality.* One would logically expect, then, that just as the conversion of the pagan Empire to Christianity justified a greater range of confidence in the legitimacy of Caesar's demands, so should the emergence of a new paganism have restored the old posture of suspicion and restraint on the part of the Christian community and its responsible leaders and guides.

As a specific instance of what I mean, let us take the familiar theological formulation which grants "the presumption of justice" in a war to the secular authority. I submit that this formulation requires a thorough re-examination of its adequacy to our time. Please note, I am not suggesting that we abandon or "revise" the fundamental moral principle that the Christian owes honor and obedience to the powers placed over him. I do insist, however, that the situation demands a very crucial change in the interpretation of this principle and its application to actual circumstances. The new interpretation could require that Caesar first prove the legitimacy of his claim to the Christian's service. More important, the Pauline "subjection to the powers" would again be one in which limits to the subjection would be recognized and even stressed.

The world is passing through a particularly tragic era marked by the extremes of totalitarian tyranny. The bitter proof of our theological inability to meet the challenge of the new paganism is the scandal that found Catholics of Nazi Germany granting "the presumption of justice" to Adolph Hitler and his infamous regime! In 1935 Archbishop Groeber of Freiburg-im-Breisgau published a treatise on "Church, Fatherland, and Love of Fatherland" in which he specifically dealt with the question of military service. Flatly rejecting the claims of pacifism, he declared, "Catholic theologians have always distinguished between the just and unjust war and have never left it to the judgment of the individual, with all of his shortsightedness and emotionality, to decide the justice or injustice of any given war. *Instead, the final decision has been left to the legitimate authority.*" (Emphasis added.)

What a grotesque irony that a moral teaching which might have held some validity in the day of the "Christian prince" should have prepared *and* obliged German Catholics to furnish active support to what may have been history's most unjust war! And the irony is reduced only slightly when we see its benefits extended to the political pragmatists (including Stalin!) making the decisions for the nations on the other side of that conflict. Given the nature and anti-Christian tone of modern war, including nuclear war; given the nature and at least non-Christian tone of the modern secular state and its rulers, I submit it is more fitting for the Christian to approach any actual or impending war under a general presumption of *injustice*. This, at least, would put the burden of proof upon the warring state and not, as is now the case, upon the individual with a troubled or doubtful conscience.

(Incidentally, if this argument holds true for participation in war, it could easily be extended to cover preparation or training for war as well. The same spiritual leaders who oblige the individual to avoid as an occasion of sin a movie which *might* induce immoral thoughts, desires and acts ought to be equally alert about obliging him to avoid a program of military training which *is designed* to induce the thought patterns and action responses that would make him less capable of judging the morality of a given war. One might also suggest that a desirable first step would be the removal of this possible "occasion of sin" from the many Catholic colleges and universities now offering such training as part of their approved curricula.)

In his criticism of an earlier paper of mine dealing with the German Catholic press and its support for Hitler's wars, George N. Shuster accurately summarized what he referred to as this writer's "thesis" that, since Catholics are forbidden to support an unjust war, it becomes the duty of Catholic spiritual leadership to proclaim the injustice of a morally indefensible war. He then made a further observation with which I fully agree, though perhaps with less equanimity than that mustered by Dr. Shuster: "I shall not comment on

117

the implications of this thesis except to say that *up to the present time it has played no part in the history of war.*" (Emphasis added.) This extremely cogent observation serves to introduce consideration of the third failing referred to above, namely, the unwillingness on the part of religious spokesmen to denounce a war in progress or under contemplation. This reticence is usually explained in terms of "prudence" as manifested in a desire to avoid making a "rash judgment" based on only partial access to the facts; a desire to avoid subjecting the Church and its individual members to the persecution that would almost certainly follow such a denunciation; and, finally, a desire to avoid placing the individual in an impossible conflict of conscience which would probably be resolved in favor of the nation's demands anyway. It is my contention that these three "desires" combine to reduce the whole structure of the "just war-unjust war" theology to the status of a patently useless and socially meaningless intellectual exercise.

This is not to say that a relevant moral theology should omit prudence from its moral equations. Quite the contrary: prudence, the virtue of doing the right thing in the right way, is an essential factor in any such equation. But this is vastly different from intentionally failing to do the right thing or using means unsuited to the proper end. Such behavior, for whatever reason, degenerates into the type of crass expediency that makes a mockery of the virtue it purports to represent.

Once again the moral dilemma of the German Catholic ordered to service in Hitler's wars is instructive. Witness, for example, the pamphlet issued by a Catholic publisher in which a theologian addressed himself to the question, "What Is To Be Done?" His advice to the Catholics for whom the pamphlet was intended was simple: This is not the time to even raise the question of the just war; instead, the only course open to the individual is to "do his best with faith in the cause of his people. A scientific judgment concerning causes and origins of the war is absolutely impossible today because the prerequisites for such a judgment are not available to us. This must wait until a later time when the documents of both sides are available." That this "later time" has now stretched to two decades

118

and, as yet, the German moralists have not issued their "scientific judgment" is not at issue here. What is at issue, though, is the basis upon which this judgment was "prudently" postponed. One must grant that any judgment based on limited access to the facts and documents risks a certain amount of "rashness," but does this justify acting under a suspension of moral judgment in the absence of such information? I think not. It might be argued that true prudence would demand taking careful note of whatever information is available and then reaching the best moral judgment possible on the basis of the incomplete information. After all, the moral theology of war must take as its starting point the inescapable fact of the Fifth Commandment; only in the case of the demonstrably just war could the question of the permissibility of taking human life in battle arise. Viewed in this context, it would seem that the more limited the access to information, the less prudent would be action contrary to the overriding authority of the Commandment and its general proscription against killing. The expert opinion cited above is obviously based on the "presumption of justice" teaching already discussed. Standing alone, it clearly violates logical order.

With particular reference now to nuclear war, the knowledge we do have concerning the weapons, their effects and the certainty of their use (even if only as a "last resort" when one or the other combatant faces imminent defeat) virtually, if not absolutely, precludes the possibility that any sufficient amount of reliable evidence could be marshaled to support such a war. This is to say that we can begin with a clear preponderance of information testifying to the war's injustice. This may still be "rash"; but it is far less so than would the grim alternative of continuing at the new level the practice of obliging Catholics on both sides of every conflict to kill their fellow members of the Mystical Body on the grounds of full or partial ignorance of the facts. The promised outcome of a nuclear war is such that any advice that we "must wait until a later time" for a "scientific judgment" of the war's justice or injustice would have a very hollow ring indeed.

The second argument from prudence, the assumed unwillingness to denounce a war because of the adverse reaction such action would bring, is difficult to reconcile with the Pauline exhortation to "preach the Word, in season and out of season." Yet, strangely enough, this is the key objection that has been raised against my critical analysis of German Catholic support for Hitler's wars. The indignation greeting the mere act of questioning the absence of German Catholic resistance to the war (*not* to the Nazi regime) leaves the impression that the meddling questioner had publicly revealed himself as totally ignorant of such elementary facts as that the Church in Hitler's Germany was continually under official suspicion of treason and treachery; that individual Catholics and their leaders would have faced a persecution similar to the one suffered by the Jews had they dared offer any organized or even widespread opposition to the war effort. Interestingly enough, the more vehement critics of my thesis apparently do not challenge my assumption that Hitler's wars were unjust; some even imply that the German bishops were aware of the injustice! Assuming these critics are right, it would mean that these eminent leaders had knowingly advised their faithful following to participate in an unjust war out of a "prudent" awareness that only in this manner could some semblance of religious life and activity be preserved under the Nazi tyranny. I frankly cannot accept so severe a judgment of the German hierarchy. I find it unthinkable that Catholic spiritual leaders, whatever their nationality, would knowingly call upon others to commit what would at least be a materially sinful act, a form of murder. It would be an unholy bargain indeed which would pay such a price for the avoidance of intensified religious persecution at home. But it is extremely significant that this defense is so openly and so frequently encountered. It testifies to a capacity on the part of those offering this defense to excuse compromise with or surrender to active participation in an unjust war as a means of escaping persecution and reprisal.

The third argument from prudence, the desire to avoid creating an "impossible conflict of conscience" and thereby risk alienating Catholics from a too-demanding Church, relates closely to the final source of what has been termed the lack of relevance in our present theological approach to the problem of modern war in general and nuclear war in particular. This was the charge that today's Christian is not being alerted to his true responsibilities and is not receiving the help and guidance he needs to ready himself for the difficult decisions and sacrifices he may be called upon to make. The criticism assumes an admittedly unpleasant contingency: simply stated, a relevant moral theology of war might impose patterns of nonconformity that could force Christianity back to the catacombs. This could follow from the retaliation on the part of a secular ruler faced with a general refusal to support an unjust war (as would most certainly have been true in Nazi Germany). Or, it could be the aftermath of national defeat resulting from such a general refusal (as conceivably might be true, let us say, if the Soviet Union were to launch an aggressive attack that could be effectively countered only by resorting to unjust means).

Father Connery, speaking of "sufficient reason," somewhat glibly posits a "quick and fatal blow" at an enemy's war machine as "the only alternative" to "the destruction of my own population." Such a tendency to dichotomize this crucial moral choice illustrates the point I am trying to make. A relevant moral theology must recognize that there are other alternatives, nonviolent forms of resistance, deserving at least some passing mention if not full and serious consideration on the part of moralists of his stature. These alternatives might not be easy to contemplate; they would almost certainly carry a heavy price in terms of prolonged physical and psychological deprivation. But they *are* alternatives.

One is immediately faced with the question: Would it be "prudent" or "realistic" to expect individual Christians to willingly accept this grim prospect of retreat to the catacombs as the alternative to participation in an unjust war? Not today, I fear. Somewhere along the centuries we became spiritually "soft." We have forgotten that the price of being a Christian was never intended to be an easy price; that, on the contrary, the closer one gets to the Cross, the closer he gets to the ideal — and the likelihood — of actual martyrdom. Self-sacrificing love of God and neighbor seems to have lost its place as the first and greatest commandment to the more practical and all-justifying "law of self-preservation." At the same time, political freedom has moved so far up the scale of ultimate values that it is almost in bad taste to refer to the fact that Christ Himself was a member of an occupied nation and the Caesar whose image was on the coin was a foreign oppressor.

These developments, too, have an important bearing upon the "state of the question."

A recent questionnaire to more than a thousand Catholic high-school students elicited virtually unanimous agreement that nuclear weapons could legitimately be used in retaliation against nuclear attack or as the "only way" to defeat communism *even if such weapons were immoral*. In its sociological statement this is a problem of value selection. Such studies and other observable behavior make it quite clear that the values associated with personal and national survival get top priority from today's Christians "when the chips are down." If, as I would certainly insist, this falls short of the Christian ideal, we are immediately faced with a task of ideological restoration: never an easy task and especially difficult in a world-setting so openly alien and even antagonistic toward the values one would have to promote. To entertain any hope for success, we must bring to this task the same clarity and firmness of purpose that marks official Catholic pronouncements on such other morally-relevant issues as birth control, divorce, condemned movies, and the wearing of bathing suits in public beauty contests.

A social therapist assigned this task of accomplishing the ideological reformation of a group or community would probably begin by finding or creating a "hero-image" to personify the value orientation he wishes to foster in individual members of the group or community. In this specific case, of course, such a hero-image is readily available in the much neglected ideal of the Christian martyr. The Catholic community continues to give tacit recognition to that ideal by regularly celebrating the feastdays of the many historic martyrs numbered in the roster of canonized saints; yet, in a more contemporary context, the image of the martyr tends to blur into that of the "extremist," the "religious fanatic" who completely estranges himself from the world of practical reality. As such, he seldom rates acceptance as a model for the ordinary Christian who prides himself on his prudent practicality. There were, for instance, some German

Catholics (extremely few!) who suffered the Nazi executioner's axe because they refused to serve in a war they considered unjust. Less than twenty years later, careful and repeated inquiry on my part failed to disclose any formal commemoration of their sacrifice on the part of the official Church in Germany. In contrast to this, I did hear of a prominent theologian who, in the course of a "Memorial Day" convocation, called upon Catholic university students to regard the German war dead of *both* world wars as models worthy of their emulation!

Realists that we are, we gladly accept the widely held "moral principle" that the Church would never (or *could* never!) require a course of action that would "force" large numbers of people or whole nations into martyrdom. Surely we come close to a modern heresy here. At the very least, this "principle" all but eliminates the ascetic content of Christianity. (Strangely enough, many who most enthusiastically proclaim this "principle" do not object when religious leaders issue hyper-nationalistic appeals for "self-sacrifice" and "martyrdom" for Folk and Fatherland!). Certainly, one could err in the other direction as well; but it would seem that the times demand greater emphasis upon the need for the Christian in our neo-pagan world to reconcile himself to the likelihood — to the *certainty* and even *desirability*, if you will — that he must suffer material, physical and psychological hardship for his faith. Wherever possible, he must discover new and morally permissible techniques of resistance to the evil forces that are abroad and must train himself in the use of these techniques with all the care and determination now lavished upon the techniques of violent resistance. And, should these new techniques prove insufficient to the task, he must abandon himself to the unfathomable will of God and be ready to die as the innocent victim of injustice, rather than save himself and those dear to him by turning to means that are immoral.

Obviously, such behavior would require far greater dedication to the ascetic ideal than we are likely to muster. To even come close requires direction and guidance, and this brings us back to the major theme of this paper: the appeal for a more relevant moral theology of war. This is essentially the appeal voiced in 1932 by Munich's

123

great Cardinal Faulhaber when he recognized the need for moral theology to "speak a new language." In doing so, he promised, "It will remain true to the old principles, but in the question of the permissibility of war, new facts will be taken into account."

Two of the "new facts" mentioned by the Cardinal involved the changes in the technology of war which had then already reached levels of destructive potential that made it "no longer human, not to mention Christian" and the consequent awareness that the aftermath of war would find the victor as much the loser as the vanquished; thereby destroying the proportionality between objectives and costs required by the traditional Catholic theology of the "just war." Unfortunately, this distinguished churchman was much too optimistic in his expectations; when the tragedy of war again enveloped the world, even he failed to speak in the new language he had promised.

The possibility of nuclear war with its certain resort to "ultimate" weapons has raised Faulhaber's "new facts" of the 1930s to even newer and then unimaginable potentialities of horror. We are still waiting — no longer quite so patiently and confidently, perhaps — for moral theology to speak its "new language." And while we wait, hope weakens. Catholics grown accustomed to a socially irrelevant theology grow ever more indifferent to the moral problem of war itself. Callousness overcomes the last lingering measure of concern as we submit our wills to pragmatic counsels of inevitability that mock all pretensions to the freedom and responsibility that once crowned the dignity of the human person.

This, I feel, is the "state of the question."

I do not think this too pessimistic an evaluation. The high-school students mentioned earlier, almost all of them products of Catholic family and parochial-school backgrounds, testify to it. Less significant statistically, but at least equally revealing, is the exchange that took place between a parochial-school teacher and the newcomer to her first-grade class. The researcher was trying to learn the extent and quality of preschool religious training in the home, and one of her questions was: "Do you know anything about God?"

This particular 6-year-old replied, "He made bombs and things bombs are made of."

124

The startled Sister decided to probe. "Why did He make those?"
"I don't know. So we could win all the wars."
"Did He make anything else?"
"I don't know."

chapter IX

Nuclear Warfare and the Law of Nations

by William V. O'Brien

O NE WAY to assess the "state" of a question of public morality is to examine the state of relevant positive law. Although differing from law in scope and character, morality underlies the law. Hence, the condition of the positive law often reveals the extent to which a judicially organized society has succeeded in applying moral principles to its specific problems. It is always possible, moreover, that an examination of positive law may reveal defects in the moral principles upon which society is relying. Studies of labor law, for example, have exposed the failure of modern societies to incorporate valid moral principles pertaining to economic and social justice into their positive laws. On the other hand, such studies have also shown what can result from application of faulty first principles, e.g., the over-enthusiastic adherence to supposedly immutable principles of nineteenth-century liberalism.

The Law of Nations

An understanding of the relation between law and morality is particularly important to the study of the normative regulation of international relations. International law is still a primitive law and, like most primitive law, it represents the efforts of a society — the international society — to translate its common moral values into rules and institutions which may be immediately applied to life within the society. I have tried to acknowledge this close interrelation of the normative disciplines of international morality and positive international law by employing the term "law of nations" in the title of this article. There is a long historical relationship between the concept of an objective natural moral law, the *jus naturale*, and the moral consensus of mankind embodied in a law of nations or "peoples," the *jus gentium* or, to the later scholastics, the *jus inter gentes*.[1] This relationship is reflected in the words for "international law" in other languages, e.g., *droit des gens, Völkerrecht*, etc., but the English term "international law" has a technical ring which implies to the layman the existence of a definite, complex body of law such as admiralty law or corporation law.

This is hardly the case with international law and even less so as regards the international law of war. It must be emphasized from the outset that there is *not* a highly developed law of war to which we may turn in solving nuclear war problems. On the contrary, it will be shown that we have only the inadequate remnant of the law of the days before the advent of total war. Nevertheless, it is important to examine this law, for it does in fact reflect a good deal about the "state of the question" of the morality of nuclear war. It reveals, among other things a historic unwillingness on the part of states to submit effective means of war to real international legal regulation based upon international morality. Examination of the relevant international law of war will also demonstrate the unfortunate effects of dependence upon supposed "first principles" which have not stood the test of practice and which are not above question in the realm of theory. This study will also, however, suggest the existence of a valid moral-legal concept which could form the basis for new efforts to subject force in the international society to normative limitation.

But, first of all what is the law of nations? Essentially it consists

---

[1] Heinrich A. Rommen, *The Natural Law*, trans. by Thomas R. Hanley, O.S.B. (St. Louis: Herder, 1949), pp. 3–75; D. P. O'Connell, "The Rational Foundations of International Law," *Sydney Law Review*, 2 (1957), 251–270.

of a body of principles, rules and institutions which states have established to govern their mutual relations. It is a law based upon custom, the conscious repetition of a pattern of behavior in international relations, resulting in general agreement that such behavior is legally required. This law is elaborated and confirmed by treaties, multilateral contractual agreements whereby states specify mutual legal rights and duties. Whether a particular rule is the product of custom alone or is specifically formulated in a treaty provision, the essence of the law of nations is that it is a law based upon *acceptance* by an effective majority of the states of the world. Although its normative validity, standards and inspiration are derived from natural law, positive international law results from the action of states. It is a law made by states, for themselves, and enforced, to the extent that it is enforced, by states.

We need not review the jurisprudential and other objections to calling the law of nations "law." As I have said, it is very primitive and it resembles only slightly the law of advanced juridical orders such as exist in modern states. The crucial point is that states, having found it neither possible nor desirable to conduct their international relations in a moral vacuum, have translated some of their concepts of international morality into particular rules and institutions of international law. It should be emphasized at this point that this translation of morality into law is as essential to the regulation of the world polity as it is to the regulation of domestic political society. We cannot operate solely on the basis of general moral principles; we must apply them by producing positive law and politico-juridical institutions to reach the problems of everyday life. This truth certainly bears upon our problem of the morality of nuclear war.

Is this law of nations not incomplete? Does it not tend to regulate the least important, most noncontroversial aspects of international life, while often leaving the crucial problems to the law of the jungle? Is it not in part based upon faulty jurisprudential and metaphysical assumptions? Is it not often hypocritically interpreted and sidestepped? Is it not frequently violated without any sanction being applied? To all, the answer is, Certainly. Does this answer mean that there is no law of nations or that, in the nature of things, there can be none? No, and it must be recalled that Catholic teaching on the subject insists not only that there *is* a law of nations but that there must be such a law which, moreover, we all have an obligation to support.

This, then, is the positive law relevant to the moral problem of nuclear warfare; the weak, primitive, maligned, but necessary and viable, law of nations. The persistence of the law of nations in the world of power politics is in itself an important fact to be considered as we confront the seemingly hopeless problems of the nuclear age.

Techniques of the Law of War

Focusing on that part of the law of nations which is concerned with war, we find that the framers of the law of war have utilized several different basic techniques in their attempts to regulate warfare. By examining the present law relative to nuclear war in terms of these techniques we can, at one and the same time, cover the substantive law and obtain some insights in the efficacy of the techniques themselves, all of which naturally figure prominently in contemporary proposals concerning restriction or abolition of nuclear war.

Essentially, there are three approaches to limiting means of war:

1. *Prohibiting certain means*: prohibiting the use of specific weapons, means, or practices of war; as we often say, "outlawing" or "banning" the thing entirely.

2. *Prohibiting certain results*: prohibiting injury to a protected class or persons or interests, regardless of the means used; for example, the deliberate injury of noncombatants or the violation of private property rights.

3. *Authorizing the use of proportionate means*: laying down positive normative guides as to how war should be conducted rather than relying exclusively on negative prohibitions indicating how it should not be conducted.

Prohibited Means

The most obvious method of dealing with a means of war to which the majority of the nations of the world object is to prohibit or outlaw it. This clear-cut, direct kind of solution has always been attractive

129

and is particularly urged as the answer to the problem of nuclear war. Occasionally this approach has produced lasting results as evidenced by such rules of the law of war as prohibition of the use of poisoned weapons, of the denial of quarter, and of pillage.[2] The fact is, however, that in the fifteen years since Hiroshima no convention outlawing or restricting the use of nuclear weapons has come close to acceptance by the nations of the world.[3] There have been proposals to shift control of existing nuclear weapons to an international authority, and proposals for the complete outlawry of nuclear weapons. All of these proposals have come to nothing, partly because of mutual distrust with respect to their implementation and enforcement and partly because of uncertainty as to their substantive merits.

Behind this fact lies another. From the attempt of the Second Lateran Council to outlaw the crossbow in 1139 to the efforts after World War I virtually to prohibit effective aerial bombardment and submarine warfare,[4] no *decisive* means of war has been successfully regulated, much less outlawed. Those means or practices of war which have in fact been prohibited by the law of war have not been of primary military importance. For example, of the three prohibitory rules mentioned above, the one prohibiting poisoned weapons concerns an archaic and unimportant means; the prohibition of denial of quarter stems from the conviction that killing unresisting enemies is a dangerous practice which usually boomerangs; and the rule against pillage is based upon the sound assumption that the practice, far from being militarily desirable, is postively harmful to military efficiency because it leads to depravity and lack of discipline among the troops.

Moreover, even with regard to relatively noncontroversial mat-

[2] Cf. Hague Convention IV Respecting the Laws and Customs of War on Land of 1907, Article 23 (a) and (d) and Article 28.

[3] One of the most serious attempts was made by the International Red Cross at New Delhi in 1957. It was a complete failure. Cf. Nineteenth International Red Cross Conference, New Delhi, January, 1957, *Draft Rules for the Limitation of the Danger Incurred by the Civilian Population in Time of War* (Geneva: International Committee of the Red Cross, 1956).

[4] For a prophetic analysis of the problems of limiting aerial bombardment as well as the best general study of legal limitation of weapons see M. W. Royse, *Aerial Bombardment* (New York: Vinal, 1928). For a comprehensive study of attempts to limit submarine warfare see William H. Barnes III, "Sub-

ters, the number of flat prohibitions in the positive law of war is very small. The great majority of the rules restricting belligerent acts have been made conditional by escape clauses permitting deviation from the rule in the event of imperative military necessity.[5] Even at the height of the movement toward regulation of the conduct of war at the end of the last century, it was hardly ever possible to obtain agreement to flat prohibitions of specific means of war; almost always the nations insisted upon the legal loophole of excepting "imperative military necessity."

Thus the experience of international-law authorities has been that sweeping prohibitions of decisive means of war have never been accepted by states and that even the prohibition of relatively minor means has usually been accepted only on condition that the rule be qualified by the exception of military necessity.

But, it will be objected, what about the successful outlawry of gas warfare? Is this not a vital exception? Moreover, does not the existing prohibition of gas clearly embrace nuclear war with its radioactive fallout? In any event, does not the experience with gas warfare prove that nuclear weapons, too, may be banned? To answer these familiar questions we must determine whether there is in fact a clear-cut legal prohibition of gas warfare, whether such a prohibition includes nuclear weapons, and just what implications may fairly be drawn from the general abstention from gas warfare since World War I.

It is controverted whether there was any law regulating or prohibiting the use of gas warfare when it first appeared in 1915.[6] In

marine Warfare and International Law," *World Polity, The Yearbook of the Institute of World Polity*, II (Washington: Georgetown University/Utrecht-Antwerp, Spectrum Publishers, 1960), 121–202.

[5] For example, Article 23 (g) of the Hague Rules of 1907 states that, ". . . it is especially forbidden . . . To destroy or seize the enemy's property unless such destruction or seizure be imperatively demanded by the necessities of war." Cf. William V. O'Brien, "The Meaning of 'Military Necessity' in International Law," *World Polity, The Yearbook of the Institute of World Polity*, I (Washington: Georgetown University/Utrecht-Antwerp: Spectrum Publishers, 1957), 109, 130–131.

[6] Cf. William V. O'Brien, "Legitimate Military Necessity in Nuclear War," *World Polity, loc. cit.*, II, 86–87; Julius Stone, *Legal Controls of International Conflict* (New York: Rinehart, 1954), pp. 553–557; Georg Schwarzenberger, *The Legality of Nuclear Weapons* (London: Stevens, 1958), p. 38.

any event, the revulsion against the gas warfare of World War I which was fairly generally felt produced the Geneva Protocol of June 17, 1925, which provided that, with respect to gas warfare, "the High Contracting Parties, so far as they are not already Parties to Treaties prohibiting such use, accept this prohibition, agree to extend this prohibition to the use of bacteriological methods of warfare and agree to be bound as between themselves according to the terms of this declaration." [7] Gas warfare was defined by the Protocol as the use in war of "asphyxiating, poisonous or other gases, and of all analogous liquids, materials or devices."

The legal effects of this broad agreement are not entirely clear. The agreement applied "as between" the contracting parties. Where did that leave noncontracting parties, such as the United States and Japan? If the Protocol was merely declaratory of previously existing law, then presumably noncontracting parties were already prohibited from using chemical warfare. The Protocol itself refers to gas warfare with expressions such as "justly condemned," but the specific form or content of this "condemnation" is not revealed. Moreover, the contractual cast of the Protocol raises the question whether violation of its provisions by one party would permit another party to retaliate with the proscribed means. Both particular interpretations of the treaty and the general law of reprisals answer that such retaliation *would* be justified. Thus, the conventional prohibition against gas warfare is not necessarily as firm and permanent as it appears to be at first glance.

But what of the impressive fact that gas warfare, which had become a standard means of war by 1918, has never been used since (with the exception of its use in Ethiopia and China). It is said that the record since 1918 supports the view that international customary law prohibits the use of gas, that this represents a major instance of international action to abolish an objectionable major means of modern warfare, and that this experience proves that the same thing is possible with regard to nuclear weapons.

The legal significance of the record with respect to gas warfare is

[7] Geneva Protocol Prohibiting Asphyxiating, Poisonous or Other Gases, and Bacteriological Methods of Warfare of June 17, 1925. Cf. Stone, *op. cit.*, pp. 553–557.

in itself a controversial question. The United States Army takes the position that neither the Geneva Protocol nor international practice have produced a binding legal prohibition against gas.[8] Moreover, the major world powers all have chemical corps which work diligently at the production of newer and better gases and germs with the result that we may be closer to serious use of chemical and bacteriological warfare today, thirty-five years after the Geneva Protocol, than ever.[9]

But even if we limit ourselves to analysis of the record of abstention from gas warfare up to the present, do we have a precedent for the successful outlawry of nuclear weapons? The answer turns on an understanding of the nature of gas warfare over the period from 1918 to the present. Gas warfare was known in 1918 to be a terrible weapon which wrought great physical and psychological suffering. But it was also notoriously unreliable. It was, in short, a destructive and disagreeable but not a *decisive* means of war which could contribute in a major fashion to winning a war. It is here that the analogy to nuclear weapons, the most decisive weapons imaginable, falls down.

The signatories to the Geneva Protocol were agreeing to the outlawry of a weapon of questionable military efficiency which had never proved to be decisive and which, on the other hand, produced suffering of a kind which general world opinion conceived to be disproportionate to any probable military advantage. Even so, the nations of the world did not trust each other to maintain the ban on gas. The early days of World War II brought scenes of frantic civilians rushing to air raid shelters wearing gas masks. Gradually the issue was put on the basis, not of complete abstention from use of gas but of not using gas *first*. This state of affairs is highly relevant to our present nuclear problems for it resembles in many ways our

[8] U.S. Department of the Army, FM 27–10, *The Law of Land Warfare* (Washington: Government Printing Office, 1956), pp. 18–19; however, a U.S. Navy publication contends that use of gas is forbidden. Cf. Robert W. Tucker, *The Law of War and Neutrality at Sea*, "Naval War College, International Law Studies, 1955, Vol. 50" (Washington: Government Printing Office, 1957), pp. 51–53.

[9] Cf. O'Brien, "Legitimate Military Necessity in Nuclear War," *op. cit.*, p. 91, for citations of articles in military publications and the press bearing out this statement.

present atomic "stalemate." Churchill and Roosevelt vowed quick retaliation in kind if the Axis powers used gas, and chemical corps preparations were pushed energetically. But apparently Hitler and his commanders could not perceive a reasonable, long-range military advantage in using their own potent gases.

The upshot is that, first, gas warfare is *not* clearly outlawed by positive international law. Secondly, the record of abstention from gas warfare cannot fairly be interpreted as providing an example of limiting a decisive, effective means of war, since gas warfare had not and has not proved itself decisive. Finally, present preparations for chemical and bacteriological war do not permit us to assume that the ban on these means would survive an opportunity for their use in such a way as to be decisive, if such use seemed to be technically feasible.

It is further believed that the argument that nuclear weapons are included in the categories of weapons supposedly outlawed by the Geneva Convention is false because it runs contrary to the whole nature of international law. The law of nations is based upon the consent of States. When grave questions of survival are involved, one would expect a rather conservative evaluation of evidence of such consent. Are we to believe that the nations of the world, whether by their adherence to the Geneva Protocol of 1925 or by their abstention from gas warfare, *consented* in advance to a prohibition against use of a decisive means of war which would not even be invented until 1945? Could it possibly have been the *intent* of the nations participating in efforts to ban gas warfare to decide in advance the fate of so novel and crucial a weapon as the atomic bomb? The answer is implicit in the whole history of man's efforts to limit the horrors of war.

Protection of Noncombatants

We turn, then, to the second basic technique of the law of war: declaring certain categories of persons or interests immune from attack or interference. There are many principles and rules of the law of war which are the product of this technique and quite a few of them bear on the problems of nuclear war.[10] However, for our purposes, it is sufficient to consider one fundamental principle which is common to the scholastic theory of the just war and positive international law: the principle of the inviolability of "innocents" or "noncombatants."[11] Father Ford, in particular, has relied upon this principle in his critiques of strategic bombing and of nuclear warfare.[12] It is not my intention to treat that principle in its moral sense and I am not primarily concerned with condemning or defending its violations in modern wars. What I do propose to show is that this principle, which was a firmly established principle of the positive law of nations, has collapsed under the pressures of modern wars, and can no longer be relied upon as a legal limitation of modern weapons. The reader must judge for himself the implications of this collapse on the "state of the question" of nuclear war and morality.

Prior to World War I, the principle that noncombatants and their property could not be the direct object of attack or injury was, in the words of John Bassett Moore, "the vital principle of the modern law of war." [13] What did this mean? It meant that people who were not in uniform, not a part of the enemy's armed forces, and not bearing arms, could not be attacked. It meant that, in general, private property was protected from arbitrary seizure or destruction. However, following the scholastic just-war doctrine, the law of nations sanctioned *unavoidable* injury to noncombatants who were unfortunate enough to be caught in an area of immediate combat. Thus, at the first battle of Bull Run, troops fought around the home of the aged, bedridden Mrs. Henry and this was morally and legally justified by the circumstances. But injury to her person or property would not have been condoned if the necessities of combat had not existed.

What happened to this great principle, demanded by chivalry, law,

[10] For a summary and analysis of these principles and rules, cf. *ibid.*, pp. 81–98.

[11] Cf. Vitoria, *De jure belli*, pars III, ques. I, prop. 2; Alfred Vanderpol, *La doctrine scolastique du droit de guerre* (Paris: Pedone, 1925), pp. 347–348.

[12] In addition to his essay in this symposium, see Father Ford's "The Morality of Obliteration Bombing," *Theological Studies*, 4 (1944), 261.

[13] John Bassett Moore, *International and Some Current Illusions and Other Essays* (New York: Macmillan, 1924), p. viii.

and morality alike? There are many explanations, some of which attribute the collapse almost entirely to the immorality of modern international society. Without prejudice to these explanations, I should like to suggest one important reason for the failure of the principle of inviolability of noncombatants. As a binding principle of the law of nations, the principle disappeared because the material conditions and the ideological assumptions which had made its application possible disappeared. First, war ceased to be fought solely with weapons, such as swords, muskets, and small cannons, which could be directly aimed and controlled and which inflicted limited damage. Long-range weapons could not distinguish between combatants and noncombatants, between military and nonmilitary targets. They were fired by calculation, often without close and accurate observation of the target area, and their area of destruction was so large that, in many instances, it was impossible to avoid injury to noncombatants and their property. Modern artillery, and later, aerial bombers and submarines, were *indiscriminate*, compared to earlier means of war. Their use in many circumstances constituted an unavoidable, intrinsic violation of the principle of inviolability of noncombatants and nonmilitary objectives. This has been true, not just since World War II, but at least since the early years of the twentieth century.

Second, the character of the societies fighting modern wars changed radically. Modern industrialized nations had to mobilize the entire society for war. In the eighteenth century it was not uncommon to find "enemy aliens" moving freely around Europe observing the grim games being carried on by rival armies, contests from which individuals might affect to hold aloof in the manner of Jean Jacques Rousseau. In modern wars no one was permitted to be aloof; the home front became, in many respects, genuinely as important as the fighting front. In the good old days one did not attack a noncombatant because, in a sense, he was not in the "game." But as early as the American Civil War armies began to attack the home front which was keeping the fighting front going.

Moreover, as war became a battle between industrial societies, between production systems, economic warfare developed in earnest and, here again, the distinction between combatants and noncombatants could not be maintained. The English merchant whose ships and cargoes were destroyed by the U-boats, the German women and children who grew weak under the British hunger blockades, the unfortunate enemy aliens whose property was confiscated — all became combatants in the total war.

Why did the noncombatants all over the world put up with this? In part, obviously, because they were persuaded that the stakes in the conflict were not the same as the stakes in the old-fashioned wars for territory and dynastic power. The common man was convinced that he was a part of the defense of his way of life, the way of life of Dixie, or of England or Germany. Indeed, he was often convinced that the defense of his nation's way of life was part of the defense of something deeper, of "democracy" or "civilization." Were these not causes worthy of the suffering of noncombatants? And was it really unreasonable to cause noncombatants on the "wrong" side to suffer if the desired result, salvation of a way of life, were achieved? [14]

This historical development raises questions which can hardly be answered here. Admittedly, there was much that was spurious in these great "crusades," and the popular justification of total-war methods was often misguided, hypocritical and immoral. Nevertheless, introduction of new, ideological, purposes into modern war raised a dilemma which we are still confronting in the nuclear age. *Some* of the ideological motivation behind recourse to war was clearly valid. There are few who contend that the destruction of the Nazi tyranny was not a reasonable, indeed an indispensable, objective. Yet to destroy Nazi Germany one had to fight; and, in the twentieth century, to fight meant to fight with means which are, as we have said, intrinsically disproportionate by the standards of previous centuries. The question is, then, is the principle of inviolability of noncombatants, in the sense that it was understood up to 1914, so immutable and unchallengeable that all wars using modern means must be immoral and illegal, no matter what the objectives or motiva-

[14] Cf. Raymond Aron, *The Century of the Total War* (New York: Doubleday, 1954); Walter Lippman, *The Public Philosophy* (Boston: Little Brown, 1955).

tion of the war? Admitting that a knight should not hack down a defenseless old woman and that a seventeenth-century cannoneer should not deliberately aim for a convent, is it so clear that it is more important to save civilian lives in Hamburg than to defeat Hitler? I am not suggesting that many of the policies pursued in the name of defeat of tyranny were not grossly exaggerated and unjustified,[15] but it would appear that an unyielding insistence on the rights of non-combatants as those rights existed before the advent of modern weapons may be neither practical nor even just.

In any event, we are concerned with the reaction of the nations of the world to this historical development of total war. That reaction may be summarized as follows:

1. The characteristic means of modern total war — long-range artillery, aerial bombardment, submarine warfare and surface blockades, economic warfare, psychological warfare, guerrilla and irregular warfare, and to an increasing extent, nuclear warfare based upon missiles — all attack the enemy society wherever it is vulnerable, without the slightest concern for noncombatant lives or interests.

2. Although the above-mentioned facts have become increasingly clear for close to fifty years, there has been no successful, indeed, no really serious effort to regulate *any* of these decisive means of modern warfare by customary or conventional international law.[16]

3. In the face of this record, international-law authorities have, with very few exceptions, gradually accepted the proposition that the principle of inviolability of noncombatants and nonmilitary targets is no longer an accepted principle of positive international law.[17]

4. The prospects for the future legal limitation of nuclear weapons are not encouraging. Despite the ebb and flow of disarmament schemes, it is fair to say that *every* state which has had the opportunity to use nuclear weapons, to prepare to use them, or to benefit

[15] Cf. Major General J. F. C. Fuller, *The Second World War* (New York: Duell, Sloan & Peace, 1949); Hanson W. Baldwin, *Great Mistakes of the War* (New York: Harper, 1949).

[16] This theme is developed by Barnes, "Submarine Warfare and International Law," *op. cit.*; O'Brien, "Legitimate Military Necessity in Nuclear War," *op. cit.* The basic work on this point remains Royse, *op. cit.*

[17] For an analysis of the literature, see O'Brien, "Legitimate Military Necessity in Nuclear War," *op. cit.*, pp. 81–84.

through their use by others, has hastened to do so. This is true of the United States, Canada, the United Kingdom, all of the members of NATO — particularly France, and even Sweden and Switzerland![18] This despite all of the condemnations of nuclear weapons since 1945.[19]

The United States Army Field Manual on the Laws of Land Warfare is quite correct, therefore, in stating: "The use of explosive 'atomic weapons,' whether by air, sea or land forces, cannot as such be regarded as violative of international law in the absence of any customary rule of international law or international convention restricting their employment."[20]

In other words, the international community has not seen fit to prepare for the possibility that efforts at disarmament and pacific settlement of disputes may fail to prevent nuclear conflict. If such conflict occurs, the state of the question of the morality of nuclear weapons will probably appear in the following light to a responsible statesman or commander: "After all of the talk, nothing was accomplished. We do not have a world federation, nor the rule of law throughout the world, nor nuclear disarmament nor any of the other things which were to be the *necessary* result of the threat of nuclear war. Now that nuclear war has come we have no positive direction whatever for the use of weapons which, whatever their morality, are not prohibited by the positive law of nations."

In these circumstances, would it not be wise to agitate for some kind of international conference to formulate rules prohibiting use of nuclear weapons, or prohibiting their use against certain objectives or under certain conditions? All that we have said thus far suggests a negative answer. Flat prohibitions and detailed rules are very difficult to achieve and even if they are agreed to in principle there remains a final complication which has proved to be the undoing of many previous attempts at this kind of solution to the problems of war. I have in mind the pernicious institution of reprisals.

[18] Cf. Klaus Knorr, *NATO and American Security* (Princeton, N.J.: Princeton University Press, 1959), particularly pp. 164, 166–167, 229.

[19] I examined the official attitudes of the major nuclear and would-be nuclear powers in "Legitimate Military Necessity in Nuclear War," *op. cit.*, pp. 75–80.

[20] FM 27–10, *op. cit.*, p. 18.

Few rights are more solidly established in the law of nations than the right of reprisal, and few principles have done so much to gloss over immoral behavior with an aura of legality. Under positive international law a belligerent has the right to retaliate against an enemy who employs illegal means. If genuinely necessary, the injured party may have recourse to otherwise illegal means, perhaps the same illegal means employed by the enemy. This exceptional right applies to all of the laws of war. It is supposed to serve two purposes: it provides a sanction for the law and it tends to restore the balance upset when one belligerent uses illegal means.

On the face of it, the right of reprisal is a reasonable and eminently necessary institution. However, it requires but a limited knowledge of modern history to recall what has gone on under the cloak of the right of reprisal. In World War I most of the flagrant violations of the existing law of neutral rights were justified as reprisals against alleged violations by the other side. By the end of the war a body of law which had been built up painfully over many years was dead. In World War II we had a ludicrous contest to establish who bombed cities *first*. It appeared that if the Germans, for example, could prove that the English actually were the first to bomb a city, then the whole Blitz was justified as a legal reprisal. On the other hand, on the grounds that the Germans "started it," the English and their Allies justified bombing German cities from 1941 through 1945.

Obviously, this kind of "legality" is ridiculous. (Unfortunately, it is not far removed from some of the facile dispositions of nuclear problems under the just-war doctrine.) If bombing cities were really contrary to the law of nations, violation of the law could not affect the legal obligation to refrain from such bombing. If it only takes one or two violations of a legal regime to collapse the whole system, then clearly the system is unsuited to its object. An *occasional* deviation from the law as a genuinely *exceptional* measure designed to enforce the law itself is one thing. But utilization of the excuse of reprisals to pull down the whole legal structure is inadmissible.

Unfortunately, experience has shown that this kind of specious "legality" abounds wherever the law itself is unrealistic, rigid, and unacceptable to its subjects. This is particularly true if it appears that the law does not take cognizance of all of the essential moral and material factors involved. Such unyielding rules of law will seldom be defied directly (at least, at first), but some excuse will be found for setting them aside; reprisals, self-preservation, imperious necessity, etc. So it is that nations might agree that certain weapons must never be used, except, of course, in justifiable reprisal. Or, noncombatants may be guaranteed protection; unless, of course, the enemy attacks your noncombatants, in which case you may slaughter his in retaliation. This kind of all-or-nothing approach to the limitation of warfare has thus far produced nothing in the way of effective positive law and this lesson cannot be ignored by those currently struggling with the moral and legal problems raised by nuclear warfare.

Legitimate Military Necessity

There remains, however, a third approach to our problem, one which has been largely overlooked but which promises to be both more realistic and more likely to serve morality than the two negative approaches. This is the positive concept of legitimate military necessity as a principle which authorizes the use of all means of war which bear a reasonable proportionality to a legitimate end.

The term "military necessity" bears the odium of thousands of loose, callous, immoral invocations. But the concept summed up in the term lies at the heart of any rational approach to war. It is a basic, unavoidable term which must be understood and applied if the conduct of war is to be placed under normative regulation.

Analyzed objectively, the term "military necessity" means exactly those things which are militarily necessary. To some this means all those things which the "military" want to do, but this does not and should not follow. What is militarily necessary is what is necessary to achieve the object of military operations and, ultimately, the object of the war. Wars are not fought as ends in themselves; they are only tools of high state policy, and their "necessities" are the means reasonably proportionate to the attainment of legitimate policy objectives.

This is already an important limitation on the conduct of war; that

141

it must not become an end in itself, that it must be subordinated to the political and moral purposes for which it is waged. But there is the further question; what, if any limitations should be imposed upon the means used for legitimate ends? Morality tells us that bad means must not be used, even for a good end. Now a means may be bad because of the circumstances of its use or it may be intrinsically bad, *malum in se*. In a sense the whole debate about the morality of nuclear war turns on the application of this fundamental moral distinction.

There are those who insist that "nuclear warfare" *in general* is *malum in se*. But it should be evident to those who have kept abreast of technological and military developments that there is, properly speaking, no such thing as "nuclear warfare" in the abstract. As Mr. Thomas Murray has shown, there are many varieties of nuclear weapons and many possible situations in which they might be used. It would seem impossible to encompass all of these variables in one moral judgment. While Professor Zahn is justified in protesting against centering the debate on nuclear war around a hypothetical attack on a warship on the high seas, one may as well object to the familiar device of assimilating all of the issues involved into the one horrible example of the attack on the New York metropolitan area. While admittedly there is a problem of "chain reactions" whereby a limited use of nuclear weapons leads to unlimited use, it is still necessary to appraise each variety of nuclear war in a specific context before passing judgment on it. In other words, we should think in terms of situations in which the use of this or that nuclear weapon would be reasonable or unreasonable, hence moral or immoral, hence justified by legitimate military necessity or not.

The essence of legitimate military necessity, therefore, is proportionality, a concept familiar to morality as well as to the various branches of positive law. Military necessity does not mean license or convenience or purposeless violence. It means controlled violence ("permissible violence," as American international-law authorities have called it) which is proportionate to legitimate ends and which is permitted by the law of nations and the natural law. To distinguish

142

this fundamental concept from other uses and abuses of the term "military necessity," I call it *legitimate* military necessity.

The function of the law of war is to apply this controlling concept to the particular incidents of war with the result that more particular principles and rules may be developed to indicate the bounds of military necessity in each area of belligerent activity: treatment of prisoners of war, occupation policies, conduct of maritime war, etc. But this cannot be done by drafting detailed codes of a priori rules. The detailed rules defining military necessity must develop, as rules developed in the common law, by precedent growing out of practice. Practice provides us with examples of the kinds of military acts which are thought to be proportionate and the kind that are condemned as disproportionate. Thus we have a rather elaborate conventional law governing the treatment of prisoners of war. This law is based upon the principles and rules which emerged from the practice of states. But, as has been shown, practice with respect to decisive means of war has not produced a consensus as to the bounds of military necessity, and when attempts were made to impose bounds by sweeping conventional rules, the result was that practice was unaffected.

Even if this analysis is accepted, however, there remains the serious problem of finding a valid basis for the establishment of guidelines of proportionality. The only practice we have with regard to nuclear war is Hiroshima, Nagasaki, and the preparations of nuclear powers for nuclear war. Unlike the common law, the law of war cannot rely on a judicial system to provide case law. Yet the fact remains that we must center our speculations about the morality and legality of nuclear warfare upon specific situations.

Normative Studies of War

The answer seems to be the case study based upon a hypothetical situation of the kind normally employed in a military maneuver or command-post exercise. On the basis of the unclassified material available, one can posit realistic situations in which nuclear weapons might be employed: in defense of NATO, in defense of Formosa,

143

in an intervention in the Middle East, in a war with the Soviet Union directly, etc. The current literature on defense policies and practices abounds with detailed discussions of the implications of our defense arrangements in different parts of the world.[21] There is no reason why moralists and legal scholars cannot address their normative analyses to these more specific expert discussions instead of remaining forever hypnotized by the "fearful choice" between *On the Beach* and *1984*. Such studies might produce the working principles and rules *de lege ferenda* upon which the international law of the future may be based.

The bridge between these speculations and studies and the practical world of the responsible decision-maker is provided by Father Murray's notion of policy guidance. As he says, the first task of the normative disciplines is to help set the proper frame of reference for the decision-making process. This normative frame of reference will be based upon the sound concepts of the doctrine of the just war — right intention, proportionality, etc. — but mere reiteration of these general principles is not enough. Basic doctrine must be elaborated and applied in terms of the complex facts of contemporary international conflict.[22]

This process, as some of the contributors to this symposium have brought out, requires the cooperative efforts of many empirical and normative disciplines. Father Murray's development of this point

[21] E.g., Knorr, *op. cit.*; Bernard Brodie, *Strategy in the Missile Age* (Princeton, N.J.: Princeton University Press, 1959).

[22] This is an appropriate place for the writer to express his indebtedness to the members of an *ad hoc* Committee on Study of Moral Problems of Contemporary International Conflict with which he collaborated in 1958–59. The Committee consisted of Dean C. J. Nuesse, Dr. William H. Roberts, Father John Courtney Murray, S.J., Dr. Heinrich Rommen, Dr. William J. Nagle and the writer. It would be impossible to identify all of the ideas and facts which the writer has received from this group as a whole and from its individual members but the influence of their thinking permeates this article.

On the subject in question, normative studies carried out against an analysis of contemporary international conflict, the writer is particularly indebted to Father Murray and Doctor Roberts. Some indication of their approach is found in Father Murray's paper in this symposium, and his contribution to *Foreign Policy and the Free Society* (New York: Fund for the Republic–Oceana Publications, 1958), pp. 21–49; and in Professor Roberts' study, "The Nature of Contemporary Conflict," *World Polity*, II, *loc. cit.*, 5–31.

constitutes perhaps the greatest of his many contributions to the nuclear debate. However, it must be admitted that even after a serious, coordinated effort has been made to marshal the facts and to weigh the values involved in a possible nuclear-war situation, there will still be room for disagreement and simple, clear-cut "answers" to our problems must not be expected. This is inherent in the nature of the complex of problems which make up the "question" of the morality of nuclear war. Failure to give unequivocal answers to this question is not, as some critics of our theologians and moralists unfairly allege, a matter of cowardice or shirking of duty. There is no sensible answer to the questions, "Is the H-bomb moral?" or "Should nuclear warfare be condemned morally?"

We must all grope on our way to tentative positions regarding nuclear war, while remaining ever-ready to modify our views if our assumptions do not hold up. My own view, for example, is that held by Father Murray, Mr. Murray, General Gavin, Dr. Kissinger, and the proponents of the "pentomic war"[23] concept in the United States Army. I am inclined to believe that some kind of limited nuclear warfare is possible and that it could be employed to defend values that ought to be defended while remaining within the limits of legitimate military necessity. Moreover, with Professor Dougherty and Father Murray, I see our future relations with communism as a life-death struggle which will end only with the defeat of one of the contestants or with the collapse of the ideological foundations of the conflict. Accordingly, I cannot put much reliance on solutions which require resolution or abatement of the conflict. Moreover I cannot accept the alternative of surrendering to communism without a fight. Yet, with Father Ford and others I reject the use of unlimited nuclear war. In these circumstances limited nuclear war seems to me to be the best way out of the dilemma posed by the threat of communist attack in the nuclear age.

Obviously any or all of these assumptions may prove unwar-

[23] Under this concept ("pent-" referring to the five principal components of planned division organization), flexibility between atomic and nonatomic firepower is the keynote of troop organization. But the effectiveness of the organization in turn depends on superiority in four vital fields — firepower, manpower, communications and mobility.

ranted. The communists may lose their determination to bury us and peaceful coexistence may prove to be more than an ephemeral tactic. Those of us who doubt that this will occur soon would, I trust, cheerfully acknowledge our error if such things were to come to pass. In my mind the more precarious assumption is the second, that some kind of limited nuclear war, which we apparently need to defend ourselves, will prove technically, politically, and militarily feasible. It may not be possible to hold the line between limited and all-out nuclear war. There is much expert opinion against limited nuclear war, but there is enough in favor of it to warrant exploring the possibilities under the mandate of Father Murray's moral imperative. Failure to do so may lead to alternatives which, while perhaps not quite as shocking as those conjured up in denunciation of nuclear war, are extremely painful and should be mentioned here.

One set of alternatives would involve some kind of resistance without nuclear weapons in the event of a communist attack. But even if we limited ourselves to World War II weapons we would be violating the strict interpretation of the principle on inviolability of noncombatants, as Father Ford has rightly said. As a matter of fact, we would have to reactivate Longstreet's cannon parked along Route 15 into Gettysburg in order to meet the pre-total war requirements of established moral and legal doctrine. Returning to the opening theme of this article, does this prove that practice is hopelessly immoral or that doctrine is not adequate for our needs; or does it prove a little of both?

But even if, for the sake of argument, we envisage a so-called "conventional," nonnuclear defense we have the difficulty that the communists will still be at liberty to use their nuclear weapons if they need them, the more so since they would not fear retaliation. Whether this state of affairs will be preferable for the people inhabiting American cities to an attempt at some kind of limited nuclear war is highly questionable. Moreover, it should be pointed out that any kind of defense, no matter how limited, will involve considerable damage to noncombatants and nonmilitary objectives. Colonel Moriarty has referred to the concern of Western Europeans over the prospects of NATO fighting a limited nuclear war in their crowded, highly industrialized area. But *any* kind of war fought in such an area will be destructive and injurious to the noncombatant populations whether it be fought with the weapons of World War II, World War I, or the Thirty Years War.

Another possibility would be to go underground and maintain guerrilla resistance after a surrender, with or without a fight, to the communists. This may be better than destroying whole cities in a single attack but neither are there, in this kind of war, real rights for noncombatants. Such wars are usually long and drawn out. They are marked by extremes of bitterness, vicious reprisals, and counter-reprisals, in which the "innocent" are usually the foremost victims. What I am trying to bring out, without losing sight of the fact that all-out nuclear warfare is unique in its destructive potentialities, is that *any* form of armed resistance to communism will be costly and will necessitate sacrifices on a large scale by innocent noncombatants.

The other set of alternatives to limited nuclear war are pacifist in nature. We would give up without armed resistance, trusting to the strength of our faith and the intercession of Providence to effect the survival of Christianity and at least some Christians. Father Murray has dealt with this viewpoint and Professor Dougherty has touched upon the implications to individual moral freedom of life under a modern totalitarian society. Like so many of the facets of our problem it is highly controversial. But in view of the tendency to concentrate on the disastrous effects of nuclear attacks it is appropriate to raise the question whether in our concern for innocent noncombatants we should account the death of a widow or infant in a nuclear war in defense of justice as a greater catastrophe than their survival in a society where the aged may be deprived of moral freedom and the young may grow up in ignorance of the fact than any such freedom could exist.

We see, then, that the alternatives (some of which have been very briefly suggested here) are all hard alternatives. There is no single satisfactory answer. But we have a moral responsibility to continue to seek the *best* answer that ingenuity and knowledge and faith can produce. In this quest we will do well to profit from the experience of centuries of efforts to regulate the conduct of war.

147

We should have learned from our brief examination of the status of nuclear weapons in the positive law of nations that any kind of moral or legal limitation on decisive means of conflict must be sought with the patience and humility appropriate to a type of undertaking which has hardly ever succeeded. This applies even more to the record of disarmament schemes than to the law of war. The more simple, clear-cut and far-reaching the solution, the more likely it is that it will not succeed. The task of diminishing the horrors of war is a complex, never-ending task which requires considerable intellectual maturity.

The task of limiting war cannot be approached in the manner of a strict teacher who raps the wrists of bad boys and lays down stern rules. The statesmen who seek to keep their nations alive in this world of conflict are not bad boys. They are men with staggering moral responsibilities to whole societies, as well as to the international common good. A bad boy may perhaps be forced to give up fighting on the way home from school, even if it means a kind of martyrdom, but a responsible statesman cannot lightly agree to "outlaw" the principal means of defense that stand between his nation and faith and his enemies who have sworn to destroy both.

The law of nations is the distilled essence of the compromises that such statesmen have found it possible to make in their nations' interests as they saw those interests. No doubt these statesmen, and the populations they represent, have been overly concerned with their national good, to the detriment of the international common good. No doubt they have been and continue to be short-sighted in their interpretations of their true national interests and in their choice of means to defend those interests. But if we try to imagine ourselves in their position we may be a bit more charitable in the inferences we make from the present state of the question of morality in the nuclear age, as reflected in the positive law of nations.

In any event, our continued discussions of this problem will be enhanced if we keep in mind that the object of our dialogue should not be the production of neat solutions expressed in sweeping moral judgments and far-reaching legal rules. We should, rather, be constantly seeking to place the problem of nuclear war in a moral perspective which will help the responsible decision-maker to make a reasonable, proportionate, and hence moral, decision. If we can contribute by our discussions to such decisions we will have contributed to the much overdue revival of the law of nations which strives, first of all, for peace, order and justice; but which governs, or ought to govern, the relations of men, even when they are engaged in armed conflict. If this seems a less attractive role than promoting an immediate world conference to solve all nuclear problems at once, let the American not forget that what his nation does in the nuclear age will, for better or for worse, have a greater impact on the law of nations of the future than a hundred such conferences.

chapter X

The Moral Problem of Modern Warfare: A Bibliography*

by Noel J. Brown

I. *Periodical Literature*

ALLISON, S. B. "Uranium and the Shape of Things to Come," *Confluence* (Cambridge, Mass.), 5 (April, 1956), 60–69.

AMRINE, MICHAEL. "New Theory of War; No More Coventrys or Hiroshimas are in Prospect; Weapons Should Make Mass Bombings Obsolete," *Catholic Digest* (St. Paul), 16 (February, 1952), 51–54.

——. "Our Submerged Hope for a Brighter World," *Bulletin of the Atomic Scientists* (Chicago), 10 (May, 1954), 156–58, 192.

AMRINE, MICHAEL and CONWAY, EDWARD A. "Open Letter to the Atomic Scientists," *America* (New York), 82 (October 15, 1949), 37–38.

——. "The Price of Our Survival," *ibid.*, pp. 12–14.

ARON, RAYMOND. "Can War in the Atomic Age Be Limited?" *Confluence* (Cambridge, Mass.), 5 (July, 1956), 99–114. Reply: R. INGRIM. *Ibid.*, p. 279.

*Editor's Note: Two considerations guided the preparation of this bibliography: (1) That the essays in this symposium can only partially reflect the "state of the question" of morality and warfare, and that the interested reader will want to go on to see what others have written. (2) That scholars stimulated to begin work on this difficult question of public morality would find a bibliography helpful. Only some of the works listed can be considered substantive contributions to the study of morality and warfare; if all the titles were significant in that sense, there would be little cause to complain that scholars and churchmen have neglected the problem.

Some of the books and articles contained in the bibliography deal only indirectly with morality; they are included because their authors discuss the political and military background against which the moral problem of modern warfare is set.

"The Atom Bomb." Letter to the Editor, *Catholic World* (New York), 177 (July, 1953), iv–v.

"Atoms and Ethics," *Times Literary Supplement* (London), 57 (June 20, 1958), 337–38.

BALDWIN, HANSON W. "Limited War," *The Atlantic Monthly* (Boston), 203 (May, 1959), 35–43.

BARCLAY, C. N. "Can World War III Start by Mistake?" *New York Times Magazine* (New York), (August 23, 1959), 11, 90–92.

BEACH, JOHN D. "Bertrand Russell Speaks for Man," *Catholic World* (New York), 181 (May, 1955), 93–98.

BEAVAN, JOHN. "Morality, Expediency and the Hydrogen Bomb," *Twentieth Century* (London), 157 (April, 1955), 297–305.

BELL, PHILIP. "Massive Preponderance. The White Paper on Defence," *Tablet* (London), 205 (February 26, 1955), 198.

BENFEY, O. T. "Nuclear Tests and Ethics," *Science* (Washington), 127 (March 14, 1958), 608.

BENNETT, JOHN C. "Official Complacency and Nuclear Tests," *Christianity and Crisis* (New York), 18 (June 9, 1958), 77–78.

———. "Preventing Nuclear War," *Social Action* (New York), 26 (December, 1959), 4–9.

BLACKETT, PATRICK M. S. "America's Atomic Dilemma," *New Statesman and Nation* (London), 47 (February 13, 1954), 180–82. Discussion: *Ibid.*, pp. 223, 253.

BRITTAIN, VERA. "British Peace Movements Today. The Coming of Nuclear Armaments Has Changed the Attitude of the Public to Peace Education," *Christian Century* (Chicago), 75 (November 19, 1958), 1334–35.

BRODIE, BERNARD. "Anatomy of Deterrence," *World Politics* (Princeton, N.J.), 11 (January, 1959), 173–91.

BUZZARD, ANTHONY W. "Graduated Deterrence — The Next Step," *Spectator* (London), 196 (March 9, 1956), 305–06. Reply: B. H. LIDDELL HART. *Ibid.*, p. 344.

———. "Limiting War," *Cross Currents* (West Nyack, N.Y.), 8 (Spring, 1958), 97–101, 128.

———. "Massive Retaliation and Graduated Deterrence," *World Politics* (Princeton, N.J.), 8 (January, 1956), 228–37.

BUZZARD, ANTHONY W., SLESSOR, JOHN and LOWENTHAL, RICHARD. "The H-Bomb. Massive Retaliation or Graduated Deterrence," *International Affairs* (London), 32 (April, 1956), 148–65.

CARY, STEPHEN G. "The Pacifist's Choice," *Worldview* (New York), 2 (August, 1959), 7–8.

CERVANTES, LUCIUS F. "Science, Theology, and the Social Order," *Homiletic and Pastoral Review* (New York), 59 (October, 1958), 25–43, esp. 29–32.

CHEADLE, G. "Morality of Warfare — A Military Problem," *Integrity* (New York), 10 (May, 1956), 8–15.

COGLEY, JOHN. "Morals and Foreign Policy," *Commonweal* (New York), 67 (January 10, 1958), 387.

———. "The Moral Trap," *ibid.*, p. 314.

———. "More on Nuclear War," *ibid.*, p. 363. Reply: BERNARD F. REILLY. *Ibid.*, pp. 433–34.

———. "Nuclear War and the Theologians," *ibid.*, p. 291. Reply: GORDON C. ZAHN. *Ibid.*, p. 386.

———. "A World Without War," *Worldview* (New York), 2 (June, 1959), 7–8.

CONNELL, FRANCIS J. "Is the H-Bomb Right or Wrong?" *Sign* (Union City, N.J.), 29 (March, 1950), 11–13(+).

―――. "Problems of War," *American Ecclesiastical Review* (Washington), 125 (July, 1951), 64–65.

―――."War Problems; Catholic Principles and Military Objectives," *ibid.*, pp. 306–07.

―――. "Weapons of Destruction," *Today* (St. Charles, Ill.), 9 (November, 1953), 10–11.

CONWAY, EDWARD A. "A-Bombs Away!" *America* (New York), 80 (January 22, 1949), 425–28.

―――. "Fear, Blackett and the Bomb," *ibid.*, p. 600.

―――. "A Moralist, a Scientist and the H-Bomb," *ibid.*, 83 (April 8, 1950), 9–11.

―――. "Pius XII on H-Bomb Tests," *Catholic Mind* (New York), 55 (November-December, 1957), 487–97.

―――. "The Race to Destruction," *Commonweal* (New York), 65 (November 16, 1956), 167–68.

COUSINS, NORMAN. "Death Comes for Tomoko," *Catholic Digest* (St. Paul), 21 (January, 1957), 11–14.

―――. "God, Man, and the H-Bomb," *Saturday Review* (New York), 37 (May 8, 1954), 22–23.

CRANE, PAUL. "Catholics and Nuclear War," *The Month* (London), 22 (October, 1959), 223–29.

CROSSMAN, R. H. S., and WIGG, G. "Dilemma of the H-Bomb," *New Statesman and Nation* (London), 49 (February 26, 1955), 268–71. Discussion: *Ibid.*, pp. 323–24, 356, 388.

Current Thought on Peace and War (New York), 1 (Winter, 1960). [A quarterly digest of literature and research in progress on the problems of world order and conflict.]

DAVIS, FRANCIS. "Peace and War: A Short Bibliography," *Blackfriars* (Oxford, now London), 30 (December, 1949), 599.

DAY, DOROTHY. "Are the Leaders Insane?" *Catholic Worker* (New York), 20 (April, 1954), 1(+).

―――. "Problems of the Pacifist," *Life of the Spirit* (London), 8 (December, 1953), 245–52.

―――. "Satan Bomb," *Catholic Worker* (New York), 16 (March, 1950), 2.

―――. "Things Worth Fighting For," *Commonweal* (New York), 48 (May 21, 1948), 136–37. Reply: H. G. THOMPSON. *Ibid.*, p. 161.

DE LA BEDOYERE, MICHAEL. "Christ in the Market Place; Christian Attitude Toward War," *Catholic Worker* (New York), 11 (November, 1944), 11.

―――. "From My Window in Fleet Street [war and Christianity]," *Catholic World* (New York), 178 (February, 1954), 377–80; 179 (July, 1954), 295–300.

―――. "How to Think About World War III," *Columbia* (New Haven), 37 (December, 1957), 11, 39–40.

DELOS, J. T. "The Sociology of Modern War and the Theory of Just War," *Cross Currents* (West Nyack, N.Y.), 8 (Summer, 1958), 248–66.

"Do Nuclear Weapons Exclude Just War?" *CAIP News* (Washington), 19 (June, 1958), 1–2.

DRAPER, GERALD. "The Idea of the Just War," *The Listener* (London), 60 (August 14, 1958), 221–23.

DRINKWATER, F. H. "A Conversation on the Hydrogen Bomb," *Blackfriars* (London), 36 (April, 1955), 114–21.

DRINKWATER, F. H. "The Morality of Nuclear War," *Commonweal* (New York), 61 (March 18, 1955), 623–27.

DRURY, GEORGE. "A Theology of War?" *Cross Currents* (West Nyack, N.Y.), 9 (Spring, 1959), 192–94.

DUN, ANGUS and NIEBUHR, REINHOLD. "God Wills Both Justice and Peace," *Christianity and Crisis* (New York), 15 (June 13, 1955), 75–78.

DWYER, ROBERT J. "Christ or Extermination," *Catholic Digest* (St. Paul), 9 (October, 1945), 75–77.

"Ère atomique et civilisation spiritualiste," *Relations* (Montreal), 10 (March, 1950), 74.

"Ethical Aspects of the Development of Atomic Energy," *Nature* (London), 158 (December 21, 1946), 889–91. Discussion: 159 (January 25–March 22, 1947), 125, 410.

"Ethics and Modern War, Urgent Moral Question," *Social Justice Review* (St. Louis), 43 (April, 1950), 18–19.

Evangelical Church in Germany. "Report of Bishop Otto Dibelius at the third ordinary meeting of the Second Synod of Evangelical Church in Germany in Berlin, April 26–30, 1958," *Ecumenical Review* (New York), 10 (July, 1958), 434–53.

FAGLEY, RICHARD M. "One Place to Hide. The Atomic Crisis and Christian Faith," *Religion in Life* (New York), 19, No. 4 (1950), 483–94.

————. "A Positive Peace Offensive," *Federal Council Bulletin* (New York), 33 (December, 1950), 16–17.

FALLAW, W. "Moral Diagnosis and Religious Cure," *Christendom* (New York), 12, No. 4 (1947), 486–97.

FERREUS (pseud.). "Courage or Perdition? The Fourteen Fundamental Facts of the Nuclear Age," *Review of Politics* (Notre Dame), 16 (October, 1954), 395–411.

FLEMING, P. "Hiroshima Questions," *Spectator* (London), 177 (December 13, 1946), 638. Discussion: *Ibid.*, pp. 674–75, 705.

FORBES, ANDREW. "The Philosophy of Destruction," *Catholic Mind* (New York), 44 (March, 1946), 171–73.

FORD, JOHN C. "The Morality of Obliteration Bombing," *Theological Studies* (Woodstock, Md.), 5 (September, 1944), 261–309.

GANNON, MICHAEL V. "Limited vs. Total War [NATO and Atomic Weapons]," *Commonweal* (New York), 68 (August 22, 1958), 510–13.

GILLIS, JAMES M. "The Atom Bomb," *Catholic World* (New York), 161 (September, 1945), 449–52.

————. "Our Threatened Values," *ibid.*, 167 (June, 1948), 201–02.

GODFREY, WILLIAM. "On Nuclear Weapons," *Tablet* (London), 211 (April 12, 1958), 349.

GOTTWALD, NORMAN K. "Niebuhr on Nuclear War," *Christian Century* (Chicago), 76 (November 11, 1959), 1311–12.

"Graduated Deterrence?" *Economist* (London), 177 (November 5, 1955), 457–58.

GRAHAM, ROBERT A. "European Catholics on War and Peace," *America* (New York), 89 (April 4, 1953), 11–14.

GREENWOOD, THOMAS. "La morale sociale et la guerre," *Relations* (Montreal), 3 (August, 1943), 203–06.

GRIFFIN, EARL B. "The Hydrogen Bomb," *Tablet* (London), 205 (June 11, 1955), 581.

HARRINGTON, M. "War and Arms," *Catholic Worker* (New York), 18 (December, 1952), 3(+).

154

HARTT, JULIAN N. "Religion and the Bomb," *Worldview* (New York), 2 (April, 1959), 7–8.

HAUER, B. "The Christian and Total Nuclear War," *Work* (Chicago), 15 (January, 1958), 8.

HEENAN, J. C. "Total War and Christianity," *Catholic Mind* (New York), 42 (January, 1944), 9–11.

HERMENS, FERDINAND A. "Politics and Ethics," *Thought* (New York), 29 (Spring, 1954), 32–50.

HILTNER, SEWARD. "Atomic Fears and Christian Courage," *Christian Century* (Chicago), 75 (March 19, 1958), 336–38.

HISLOP, IAN, BRIGHT, LAURENCE and EVANS, ILLTUD. "The Morality of Nuclear War," *Blackfriars* (London), 37 (March, 1956), 100–17.

HOLLIS, CHRISTOPHER. "The End of the World. Theology and the Atomic Age," *Tablet* (London), 191 (February 28, 1948), 131.

———. "Strength out of Weakness," *Spectator* (London), 202 (May 1, 1959), 609.

HOMRIGHAUSEN, E. G. "The H-Bomb Explodes," *Theology Today* (Princeton, N.J.), 11 (July, 1954), 277–79.

HORTON, MILDRED C. "The Churches' Neglected Opportunity," *National Council Outlook* (New York), 6 (June, 1956), 5–7.

HULA, ERICH. "The Revival of the Idea of Punitive War," *Thought* (New York), 21 (September, 1946), 405–34.

JACKSON, DON. "Atom Bomb: What Next?" *Christian Science Monitor Magazine* (Boston), (October 13, 1945), 5.

JERROLD, DOUGLAS. "A World in Disorder. Fruits of a Moral Abdication," *Tablet* (London), 201 (January 3, 1953), 4–5.

JOYCE, JAMES AVERY. "The Moral Deterrent," *Nation* (New York), 185 (July 6, 1957), 11–13.

KAY, LILLIAN WALD and GITLIN, IRVING J. "Atomic Energy or the Atomic Bomb: A Problem in the Development of Morale and Opinion," *Journal of Social Psychology* (Provincetown, Mass.), 29 (February, 1949), 57–84.

KEAN, CHARLES D. "The Bomb Under God," *Christian Century* (Chicago), 73 (October 17, 1956), 1199–201.

KENNAN, GEORGE F. "Foreign Policy and the Christian Conscience," *The Atlantic Monthly* (Boston), 203 (May, 1959), 44–49.

KOTANI, HIDEJIRO. "International Morality in the Nuclear Age," *Journal of International Affairs* (New York), 12 (1958), 216–21.

LEFEVER, ERNEST W. "The Ethics of Calculation," *Worldview* (New York), 2 (October, 1959), 6–8. Correspondence: 2 (November, 1959), 7–8.

LEGUEY-FEILLEUX, JEAN-ROBERT. "The Law of War: A Bibliography, 1945–1958," *World Polity* (Washington), 2 (1960), 319–414.

LEVY, J. "God Helps Him Who Helps Himself. A Philosophical Dialogue Occasioned by the Hydrogen Bomb," *Hibbert Journal* (London), 53 (April, 1955), 238–46.

LINDEMAN, EDUARD C. "Morality for the Atomic Age," *Forum* (Philadelphia), 104 (November, 1945), 231–33.

LUMBRERAS, PETER. "Morality of the A-Bomb," *Catholic Mind* (New York), 53, (May, 1955), 265–69.

MCCARTHY, JOHN. "The Morality of the Hydrogen Bomb as a War Weapon," *Irish Ecclesiastical Record* (Dublin), 74 (October, 1950), 358–63.

MCCLEERY, ROBERT S. "A Christian Answer to Atomic War," *Bulletin of the Atomic Scientists* (Chicago), 12 (September, 1956), 276–77. Reply: LEO F. KOCH. 13 (January, 1957), 40–41.

155

McHUGH, L. C. "Mute in the Face of Horror?" *America* (New York), 100 (October 18, 1958), 62.

McREAVY, LAWRENCE L. "An Anglican Verdict on the Atomic Bomb," *Clergy Review* (London), 30 (July, 1948), 1–10.

———. "Conscience and the H-Bomb," *Catholic World* (New York), 187 (July, 1958), 246–51.

———. "Morality and Nuclear War," *Commonweal* (New York), 68 (June 6, 1958), 246–49.

MAHONEY, E. J. "Ethical Aspect of the Atomic Bomb," *Clergy Review* (London), 25 (October, 1945), 475–76.

MALIK, C. H. "Ultimate Questions," *Catholic Worker* (New York), 21 (March, 1955), 3(+).

MARTIN, THOMAS OWEN. "Problems in the Morality of Warfare," *Catholic Theological Society of America Proceedings* (Washington), 2 (1947), 47–71.

MEACHAM, STEWART. "Arms and Christian Responsibility," *Christian Century* (Chicago), 76 (August 5, 1959), 896–99.

MILLER, WILLIAM LEE. "Misplaced Morality," *Worldview* (New York), 1 (January, 1958), 7–9. Correspondence: ROBERT HAVIGHURST and GORDON POTEAT. 1 (March, 1958), 9. WILLIAM A. BANNER. "Moral Concern," 1 (June, 1958), 8.

MILLIS, WALTER. "Ultimate Weapons — Ultimate Questions," *New York Times Magazine* (New York), (April 14, 1957), 9, 67–70.

MILLS, C. WRIGHT. "A Pagan Sermon to the Christian Clergy," *Nation* (New York), 186 (March 8, 1958), 199–202.

MONTGOMERY, BERNARD LAW. "The Panorama of Warfare in a Nuclear Age," *Journal of the Royal United Service Institution* (London), 101 (November, 1956), 503–20.

"Morals and the Bomb," *Commonweal* (New York), 51 (October 28, 1949), 59–60.

"Morals and the H-Bomb," *America* (New York), 83 (May 27, 1950), 256.

"Morals in War," *Catholic Mind* (New York), 48 (January, 1950), 49–50.

"Moral Teachings on Nuclear War," *Tablet* (London), 211 (March 22, 1958), 266.

MORSE, MARSTON. "Holy See and the Atom," *Social Order* (St. Louis), 7 (February, 1957), 95–96.

MORTON, DESMOND. "Morality in International Relations," *Blackfriars* (London), 36 (April, 1955), 108–13.

MUMFORD, LEWIS. "How War Began," *Saturday Evening Post* (Philadelphia), 231 (April 18, 1959), 24, 72–77.

———. "The Morals of Extermination," *The Atlantic Monthly* (Boston), 204 (October, 1959), 38–44.

MURPHY, FRANCIS X. "God, Man and the Atom Bomb," *Catholic World* (New York), 163 (May, 1946), 144–51.

MURPHY, GARDNER. "Face Those Atomic Fears!" *Christian Century* (Chicago), 75 (February 26, 1958), 250–51.

MURRAY, THOMAS E. "Rational Nuclear Armament," *Catholic Mind* (New York), 55 (September–October, 1957), 387–97.

———. "Reliance on H-Bomb and Its Dangers," *Life Magazine* (New York), (May 6, 1957), 181–98.

MUSTE, A. J. "The H-Bomb as Deterrent," *Christianity and Crisis* (New York), 14 (June 14, 1954), 77–79.

MUSTE, A. J. "The Moral Limits of War," *Nation* (New York), 181 (August 6, 1955), 117.

NIEBUHR, REINHOLD. "The Cold War and the Nuclear Dilemma," *Cross Currents* (West Nyack, N.Y.), 9 (Summer, 1959), 212–24.

———. "Nuclear War and the Christian Dilemma," *Theology Today* (Princeton, N.J.), 15 (January, 1959), 542–43.

"Nuclear War." Letters to the Editors by EDWARD T. GARGAN and GORDON C. ZAHN, *Commonweal* (New York), 68 (April 25, 1958), 107–08.

O'BRIEN, WILLIAM V. "Legitimate Military Necessity in Nuclear War," *World Polity* (Washington), 2 (1960), 35–120.

———. "The Meaning of 'Military Necessity' in International Law," *ibid.*, 1 (1957), 109–76.

———. "Nuclear War and International Law and Morality," *Foreign Service Courier* (Washington), 8 (February 19, 1960), 8–11, 14–17.

———. "The Role of Force in the International Juridical Order," *The Catholic Lawyer* (Brooklyn, N.Y.), 6 (Winter, 1960), 22–32, 47.

OLSON, GEORGE L. "Let It Not Be Again!" *Christian Century* (Chicago), 76 (December 9, 1959), 1445.

O'SULLIVAN-BARRA, J. "Morality of Warfare — A Theological Problem," *Integrity* (New York), 10 (May, 1956), 16–25.

———. "Without Mercy," *ibid.*, 8 (June, 1954), 18–26.

OTTAVIANI, ALFREDO. "The Future of Offensive War," *Blackfriars* (Oxford, now London), 30 (September, 1949), 415–20.

PEPLER, CONRAD. "War in Tradition and Today," *Blackfriars* (London), 35 (February, 1954), 62–67.

PFAFF, WILLIAM. "Two Kinds of War," *Commonweal* (New York), 58 (June 26, 1953), 300–02.

PIUS XII. Address to the Pontifical Academy of Sciences (February 8, 1948), *Catholic Documents* (London), 1 (Epiphany, 1950), 3–10.

———. Allocution to the Ambassador of Ecuador (July 13, 1948), *Acta Apostolicae Sedis* (Vatican City), 40 (1948), 339–40.

———. "Ban on ABC Warfare." Easter Message, 1954, *Catholic Mind* (New York), 52 (July, 1954), 438–40.

———. "The Cause of Peace." Allocution to the Thirteenth International Congress of the World Union of Organizations of Catholic Women (April 24, 1952), *ibid.*, 50 (July, 1952), 441–45.

———. "The Challenge of Science." Allocution to the Pontifical Academy of Sciences (April 24, 1955), *Tablet* (London), 205 (June 11, 1955), 570–71.

———. Christmas Eve Address (1951), *Catholic Mind* (New York), 50 (April, 1952), 248–56.

———. Christmas Eve Address (1953), *ibid.*, 52 (March, 1954), 174–83.

———. Christmas Message (1944), *ibid.*, 43 (February, 1945), 65–77.

———. Christmas Message (1948), *ibid.*, 47 (March, 1949), 179–87.

———. Christmas Message (1954), *American Ecclesiastical Review* (Washington), 132 (February, 1955), 123–38.

———. Christmas Message (1956), *Catholic Mind* (New York), 55 (March–April, 1957), 165–82.

———. Easter Message (1955), *ibid.*, 53 (July, 1955), 431–33.

———. Easter Message (1956), *ibid.*, 54 (June, 1956), 345–49.

———. "Man's Peace and Security." Christmas Message (1955), *Vital Speeches* (New York), 22 (January 15, 1956), 194–99.

———. "Medical Ethics." Allocution to the Eighth Congress of the World

157

Medical Association (September 30, 1954), *Catholic Mind* (New York), 53 (April, 1955), 242–52.

PIUS XII. "Medical Ethics and Law; an Address by His Holiness to the International Office of Documentation for Military Medicine (October 19, 1953)," *ibid.*, 52 (January, 1954), 46–54.

———. "The Strength of the Church." Allocution to the College of Cardinals for the Feast of St. Eugene, *Tablet* (London), 187 (June 8, 1946), 292–93.

———. "Warfare and Military Life." Allocution to the Patronesses for Spiritual Assistance to the Italian Armed Forces (May 21, 1958), *The Pope Speaks* (Washington), 5 (Summer, 1958), 41–44.

———. "Who Are to Be the Architects?" Radio Address on the Fifth Anniversary of the Outbreak of War, *Tablet* (London), 184 (September 9, 1944), 124–26.

Protestant Federation of France, The Committee for Ecumenical Studies. "Christians and the Prevention of War in the Atomic Age," *Cross Currents* (West Nyack, N.Y.), 9 (Winter, 1959), 21–29.

RAMSEY, PAUL. "The Politics of Fear. The Possible Effects of Modern War Must Not Reduce Us to Inaction," *Worldview* (New York), 3 (March, 1960), 4–7.

———. "Right and Wrong Calculation," *ibid.*, 2 (December, 1959), 6–9.

"Religion and the Present Time," *Worldview* (New York), 1 (April, 1958), 1–2.

REYNOLDS, ROBERT L. "The Church and Peace," *Jubilee* (New York), 2 (December, 1954), 10–17.

RICHARDS, G. C. T. "Moral Problems of War and Victory," *Journal of the Royal United Service Institution* (London), 101 (November, 1956), 559–67.

ROBERTS, T. D. "Nuclear Dilemma," *Month* (London), 19 (May, 1958), 282–86.

ROBERTS, WILLIAM H. "The Nature of Contemporary Conflict," *World Polity* (Washington), 2 (1960), 9–34.

ROWE, W. C. "Ethics of Surrender," *Infantry Journal* (Washington), 58 (April, 1946), 24–26.

RYAN, J. K. "Unlimited War and Traditional Morality," *Modern Schoolman* (St. Louis), 22 (November, 1944), 24–32.

SANDELL, WARREN. "The Church and Nuclear Warfare," *Church Quarterly Review* (London), 159 (April–June, 1958), 256–65.

SCHOMER, HOWARD. "Christian Non-Violence in the Nuclear Age," *Social Action* (New York), 26 (December, 1959), 10–17.

SCHWARZSCHILD, STEVEN S. "Theologians and the Bomb," *Worldview* (New York), 2 (May, 1959), 7–8.

SHEED, WILFRID. "The Christian and the H-Bomb," *Jubilee* (New York), 7 (August, 1959), 52–55.

SHEERIN, JOHN B. "A Pagan Sermon on the H-Bomb [by C. Wright Mills]," *Catholic World* (New York), 187 (June, 1958), 163–64.

SPINKS, G. S. "World Conscience and the Hydrogen Bomb," *Hibbert Journal* (London), 48 (July, 1950), 334–38.

"State and War and the Popes," *Catholic Worker* (New York), 14 (May, 1948), 6; (June, 1948), 6.

"Statement on Atomic Tests and Disarmament," *Ecumenical Review* (New York), 10 (October, 1957), 70–72.

STOWELL, ELLERY C. "The Laws of War and the Atomic Bomb," *American Journal of International Law* (Washington), 39 (1945), 784–88.

158

STRATMANN, FRANZISKUS. "War and Christian Conscience," *Cross Currents* (West Nyack, N.Y.), 3 (Winter, 1953), 107–17.

STRAUSZ-HUPE, ROBERT. "On War and Peace," *Review of Politics* (Notre Dame), 16 (October, 1954), 485–94.

STURZO, LUIGI. "The Influence of Social Facts on Ethical Conceptions," *Thought* (New York), 20 (March, 1945), 97–116.

"Swords and Ploughshares," *Tablet* (London), 207 (May 5, 1956), 413–14.

THOMPSON, CHARLES S. "The Notion of a Just War," *Tablet* (London), 208 (November 10, 1956), 410–11.

THOMPSON, KENNETH W. "American Approaches to Moral Choice," *Worldview* (New York), 1 (October, 1958), 3–5.

———. "Moral Choices in Foreign Affairs," *ibid.*, (September, 1958), 4–7.

THOMSON, G. "Hydrogen Bombs: The Need for a Policy," *International Affairs* (London), 26 (October, 1950), 463–69. Discussion: 27 (January-April, 1951), 134–35, 270–71.

TODD, JOHN M. "Just Wars and Christian Peace," *Irish Ecclesiastical Record* (Dublin), 83 (January, 1955), 27–40.

TOMLIN, E. W. F. "Atomic Energy and the Order of Nature," *Confluence* (Cambridge, Mass.), 5 (April, 1956), 45–59.

WALSH, EDMUND A. "May We Use the A-Bomb First?" *Catholic Digest* (St. Paul), 15 (August, 1951), 1–5.

WALSH, KEVIN. "Nuclear War," *Commonweal* (New York), 65 (March 22, 1957), 641–42.

"War and Peace. A Discussion of the World's Most Pressing Problem from the Moral Viewpoint," *Jubilee* (New York), 4 (April, 1957), 15–21. Discussion: 5 (June, 1957), 5–6.

"War Without Suicide," *Economist* (London), 184 (August 24, 1957), 615–16.

WATKIN, E. I. "Unjustifiable War," *Cross Currents* (West Nyack, N.Y.), 9 (Summer, 1959), 225–32.

WEIGEL, GUSTAVE. "How Relevant is Morality? And How Can it Speak to World Affairs?" *Worldview* (New York), 1 (April, 1958), 4–7.

WEINSTEIN, A. "Security Without Suicide," *Spectator* (London), 196 (March 9, 1956), 306–09.

WILHELMSEN, FREDERICK D. "Christian Pacifism: An Orthodox View. The Non-Violence Position Represents a Principled Refusal to Look at Reality," *Worldview* (New York), 3 (April, 1960), 3–5.

ZAHN, GORDON C. "The A-Bomb: Moral or Not?" *Commonweal* (New York), 52 (September 29, 1950), 606–07. Reply: FRANCIS J. CONNELL. 52 (September 29, 1950), 607–08. Discussion: 53 (November 3, 1950), 93–94.

———. "An Island Disappears [Problems of the American Catholic Attitude Toward the Use of Atomic Weapons and Other Modern Weapons]," *Catholic World* (New York), 177 (May, 1953), 107–13.

ZAMAYON, PELAYO. "Morality of War Today and in the Future," *Theology Digest* (St. Marys, Kan.), 5 (Winter, 1957), 2–5.

II. *Books and Pamphlets*

ADDISON, JAMES THAYER. *War, Peace and the Christian Mind. A Review of Recent Thought.* Foreword by HENRY KNOX SHERRILL. Greenwich, Conn.: Seabury, 1953.

AMRINE, MICHAEL. *The Great Decision: The Secret History of the Atomic Bomb.* New York: Putnam, 1959.

APPADORAI, ANGADIPURAM. *The Use of Force in International Relations.* Bombay: Asia Publishing House, 1958.

ARNOTT, DAVID GEORGE. *Our Nuclear Adventure, Its Possibilities and Perils.* New York: Philosophical Library, 1958.

ARON, RAYMOND. *The Century of Total War.* Garden City, N.Y.: Doubleday, 1954.

———. *On War. Atomic Weapons and Global Diplomacy.* Translated from the French by TERENCE KILMARTIN. London: Secker & Warburg, 1958.

———. *War and Industrial Society.* London: Oxford Univ. Press, 1958.

The Atomic Age ("Sir Halley Stewart Lectures, 1948"). BLACKETT, PATRICK M. S. "Military Consequences of Atomic Energy"; RUSSELL, BERTRAND. "Values in the Atomic Age"; CURTIS, LIONEL. "The Political Repercussions of Atomic Power"; and other lectures. London: Allen and Unwin, 1949.

BALDWIN, HANSON W. *The Great Arms Race.* New York: Praeger, 1958.

———. *Power and Politics. The Price of Security in the Atomic Age.* Claremont, Cal.: Claremont College, 1950.

BENNETT, JOHN COLEMAN. *Christians and the State.* New York: Scribner, 1958.

BIGELOW, ALBERT. *The Voyage of the Golden Rule. An Experiment With Truth.* Garden City, N.Y.: Doubleday, 1959.

BIORKLUND, ELIS. *International Atomic Policy During a Decade. An Historical-Political Investigation into the Problem of Atomic Weapons During the Period 1945–1955.* Trans. in Stockholm by ALBERT READ in cooperation with the author. London: Allen and Unwin, 1956.

BLACKETT, PATRICK M. S. *Atomic Weapons and East-West Relations.* Cambridge: Cambridge Univ. Press, 1956.

———. *Fear, War, and the Bomb.* New York: Whittlesey, 1949.

BONDURANT, JOAN VALERIE. *Conquest of Violence. The Gandhian Philosophy of Conflict.* Princeton, N.J.: Princeton Univ. Press, 1958.

BOWETT, D. W. *Self-Defense in International Law.* New York: Praeger, 1958.

British Council of Churches. *Christians and Atomic War: A Discussion of the Moral Aspects of Defence and Disarmament in the Nuclear Age.* London: British Council of Churches, 1959.

———. *The Church and the Atom. A Study of the Moral and Theological Aspects of Peace and War.* Report of a Commission appointed by the Archbishops of Canterbury and York at the request of the Church Assembly to consider the report of the British Council of Churches' Commission entitled *The Era of Atomic Power,* and to report. London (Westminster): Press and Publications Board of the Church Assembly, 1948.

———. *The Era of Atomic Power.* Report of a Commission appointed by the British Council of Churches. London: S. C. M., 1946.

BRODIE, BERNARD. *The Anatomy of Deterrence.* Santa Monica, Cal.: RAND Corp., 1958.

———. *Implications of Nuclear Weapons in Total War.* Santa Monica, Cal.: RAND Corp., 1957.

———. *The Meaning of Limited War.* Santa Monica, Cal.: RAND Corp., 1958.

———. *Strategy in the Missile Age.* Princeton, N.J.: Princeton Univ. Press, 1959.

BRODIE, BERNARD (ed.), WOLFERS, ARNOLD, CORBETT, PERCY E., AND FOX, WILLIAM T. R. *The Absolute Weapon. Atomic Power and World Order.* New Haven, Conn.: Yale Institute of International Studies, 1946.

BROWN, HARRISON SCOTT. *Must Destruction Be Our Destiny?* New York: Simon and Schuster, 1946.

BURHOP, ERIC H. S. *The Challenge of Atomic Energy*. London: Lawrence & Wishart, 1951.

BURNS, ARTHUR LEE. *Power Politics and the Growing Nuclear Club*. Princeton, N.J.: Center of International Studies, Woodrow Wilson School of Public and International Affairs, Princeton University, 1959.

BUSH, VANNEVAR. *Modern Arms and Free Men. A Discussion of the Role of Science in Preserving Democracy*. New York: Simon and Schuster, 1949.

BUTTERFIELD, HERBERT. *Christianity, Diplomacy and War*. New York: Abingdon-Cokesbury, 1953.

————. *International Conflict in the Twentieth Century. A Christian View*. New York: Harper, 1960.

CALHOUN, MALCOLM P. (ed.). *Christians are Citizens. The Role of the Responsible Christian Citizen in an Era of Crisis*. Richmond: Published for the Board of Church Extension, Presbyterian Church in the United States by John Knox Press, 1957.

Catholic Association for International Peace. *The Morality of Conscientious Objection to War*. Report by Cyprian Emanuel, O.F.M., and the CAIP Committee on Ethics. Washington: The Catholic Association for International Peace, 1941.

————. *A Papal Peace Mosaic, 1878–1944. Excerpts from the Messages of Popes Leo XIII, Pius X, Benedict XV, Pius XI, and Pius XII*. Compiled by Rev. HARRY C. KOENIG. Washington: The Catholic Association for International Peace; New York: Paulist, 1944.

————. *Peace in the Atomic Age*. Washington: The Catholic Association for International Peace, 1947.

CHESTNUT, D. LEE. *The Atom Speaks, and Echoes the Word of God*. Grand Rapids: Eerdmans, 1951.

CLAIR, FREDERIC F. *The Ultimate Defense. A Practical Plan to Prevent Man's Self-Destruction*. Rutland, Vt.: Bridgeway, 1959.

COLLINS, LEWIS JOHN and GOLLANCZ, VICTOR. *Christianity and the War Crisis*. London: Gollancz, 1951.

COUSINS, NORMAN. *Modern Man Is Obsolete*. New York: Viking, 1945.

CROWTHER, JAMES GERALD and WHIDDINGTON, R. *Science at War*. New York: Philosophical Library, 1948.

DARNLEY, ESME IVO BLIGH. *Man's Last Chance*. London: Dakers, 1947.

DINERSTEIN, HERBERT SAMUEL. *War and the Soviet Union. Nuclear Weapons and the Revolution in Soviet Military and Political Thinking*. New York: Praeger, 1959.

DONNELLY, CHARLES H. *Current Strategic Thinking as to Future Wars*. Washington: Library of Congress, Legislative Reference Service, 1957.

————. *United States Defense Policies in 1957*. 85th Congress, 2nd Session, House Document No. 436. Washington: U.S. Government Printing Office, 1958.

————. *United States Defense Policies since World War II*. Washington: U.S. Government Printing Office, 1957.

Federal Council of the Churches of Christ in America. *The Christian Conscience and Weapons of Mass Destruction*. Report of a Special Commission appointed by the Federal Council of the Churches of Christ in America, Department of International Justice and Goodwill. New York: Federal Council of the Churches of Christ in America, 1950.

Federal Council of the Churches of Christ in America, Commission on the Relation of the Church to the War in the Light of the Christian Faith.

Atomic Warfare and the Christian Faith, Report. New York: Federal Council of the Churches of Christ in America, 1946.

GARTHOFF, RAYMOND L. *The Soviet Image of Future War.* Washington: Public Affairs, 1959.

———. *Soviet Strategy in the Nuclear Age.* New York: Praeger, 1958.

GAVIN, JAMES MAURICE. *War and Peace in the Space Age.* New York: Harper, 1958.

GIACOMELLI, RAFFAELE. *Atom Bomb and Mass Destruction.* Rome: Editoriale aeronautico, 1947.

GIGON, FERNAND. *Formula for Death, E=MC². The Atom Bombs and After.* Trans. from the French by CONSTANTINE FITZ GIBBON. New York: Roy, 1958.

GLOVER, EDWARD. *War, Sadism and Pacifism. Further Essays on Group Psychology and War.* London: Allen and Unwin, 1947.

GODDARD, HAROLD CLARKE. *Atomic Peace.* Wallingford, Pa.: Pendle Hill, 1951.

GOLLANCZ, VICTOR. *The Devil's Repertoire; or, Nuclear Bombing and the Life of Man.* Garden City, N.Y.: Doubleday, 1959 [1958].

GONELLA, GUIDO. *The Papacy and World Peace. A Study of the Christmas Messages of Pope Pius XII.* London: Hollis & Carter, 1945.

GREGG, RICHARD BARTLETT. *The Power of Nonviolence.* 2nd rev. ed. Nyack, N.Y.: Fellowship Publications, 1959.

HALLE, LOUIS JOSEPH. *Choice for Survival.* New York: Harper, 1958.

HERZ, JOHN H. *International Politics in the Atomic Age.* New York: Columbia Univ. Press, 1959.

HILL, NORMAN LLEWELLYN, and LUND, DONIVER A. *If the Churches Want World Peace.* New York: Macmillan, 1958.

HUGHES, EMMET J. *America the Vincible.* Garden City, N.Y.: Doubleday, 1959.

HUTCHINS, ROBERT MAYNARD. *The Atomic Bomb Versus Civilization.* Washington and Chicago: Human Events, 1945.

India (Republic). Parliament. House of the People. *Atomic and Hydrogen Weapons. Comments and Reactions, 1954–1955.* New Delhi: Lok Sabha Secretariat, 1956.

JUNGK, ROBERT. *Brighter Than a Thousand Suns. The Moral and Political History of the Atomic Scientists.* Trans. by JAMES CLEUGH. London: Gollancz, 1958.

KAEMPFFERT, WALDEMAR. et al. *America's Atomic Bomb: What Shall We Do With It?* New York: World Peaceways, Inc., 1945.

KAHN, HERMAN. *The Nature and Feasibility of War and Deterrence.* Santa Monica, Cal.: RAND Corp., 1960.

KAPLAN, MORTON A. *The Strategy of Limited Retaliation.* Princeton, N.J.: Center of International Studies, Woodrow Wilson School of Public and International Affairs, Princeton University, 1959.

KAUFMANN, WILLIAM W. *The Requirements of Deterrence.* Princeton, N.J.: Center of International Studies, Princeton University, 1954.

KAUFMANN, WILLIAM W. (ed.). *Military Policy and National Security.* Princeton, N.J.: Princeton Univ. Press, 1956.

KECSKEMETI, PAUL. *Strategic Surrender. The Politics of Victory and Defeat.* Stanford, Cal.: Stanford Univ. Press, 1958.

KENDALL, WILLMOORE, and SIBLEY, MULFORD Q. *War and the Use of Force: Moral or Immoral, Christian or Unchristian. A Debate at Stanford University.* Denver: Swallow Press, 1959.

KENNAN, GEORGE F. *Russia, the Atom and the West*. New York: Harper, 1958.
KING-HALL, STEPHEN. *Defense in the Nuclear Age*. Nyack, N.Y.: Fellowship Publications, 1959.
KISSINGER, HENRY A. *Nuclear Weapons and Foreign Policy*. New York: Harper, 1957.
KNOX, RONALD A. *God and the Atom*. New York: Sheed & Ward, 1945.
LANG, DANIEL. *From Hiroshima to the Moon. Chronicles of Life in the Atomic Age*. New York: Simon and Schuster, 1959.
LAPP, RALPH EUGENE. *Must We Hide?* Cambridge, Mass.: Addison–Wesley Press, 1949.
LEFEVER, ERNEST W. *Ethics and United States Foreign Policy*. New York: Meridian, 1957.
LOCKYER, HERBERT. *The H-Bomb and the End of the Age*. Grand Rapids: Zondervan, 1950.
LONG, EDWARD LE ROY. *The Christian Response to the Atomic Crisis*. Philadelphia: Westminster, 1950.
———. *Religious Beliefs of American Scientists*. Philadelphia: Westminster, 1952.
———. *Science and Christian Faith. A Study in Partnership*. New York: Association, 1950.
MCALLISTER, GILBERT (ed.). *The Bomb: Challenge and Answer*. London: Batsford, 1955.
MACGREGOR, GEORGE H. C. *The New Testament Basis of Pacifism*. New and rev. ed. London: Fellowship of Reconciliation, 1953.
Mid-West Debate Bureau. *International Control of Nuclear Weapons. Resolved: That the Further Development of Nuclear Weapons Should Be Prohibited by International Agreement*. Normal, Ill., 1958.
MILLIS, WALTER, and MURRAY, JOHN COURTNEY. *Foreign Policy and the Free Society*. New York: Published for the Fund For the Republic by Oceana Publications, 1958.
MILLS, C. WRIGHT. *The Causes of World War III*. New York: Simon and Schuster, 1958.
MOCH, JULES. *Human Folly: To Disarm or Perish?* Translated by EDWARD HYAMS, with an introduction by ALBERT EINSTEIN. London: Gollancz, 1955.
MOELLERING, RALPH LUTHER. *Modern War and the American Churches. A Factual Study of the Christian Conscience on Trial from 1939 to the Cold War Crisis of Today*. New York: American, 1956.
MORRISON, CHARLES CLAYTON. *The Christian and the War*. Chicago, New York: Willett Clark, 1942.
MUMFORD, LEWIS. *Atomic War — The Way Out*. London: National Peace Council, 1948.
———. *The Human Way Out*. Wallingford, Pa.: Pendle Hill, 1958.
———. *Programme for Survival*. London: Secker & Warburg, 1946.
MURRAY, THOMAS E. *Nuclear Policy for War and Peace*. Cleveland and New York: World, 1960.
———. *The Predicament of Our Age. The Impact of the Atom on the Relationship Between Man and the World in Which He Lives*. New York: [Privately published], 1955.
NASSAR ZACARIAS, RICARDO. *El derecho internacional ante la bomba atomica*. Mexico City: Universidad Nacional Autónoma de México, 1954.
National Council of Churches. *Theological and Moral Considerations in International Affairs*. Background paper prepared by John Bennett for the

Fifth World Order Study Conference of the National Council of Churches (Cleveland, 1958). New York: National Council of Churches, 1958.

National Planning Association. Special Project Committee on Security Through Arms Control. *1970 Without Arms Control. Implications of Modern Weapons Technology.* Planning Pamphlet No. 104. Washington: National Planning Association, 1958.

————. *The Nth Country Problem and Arms Control.* A statement by the NPA Special Project Committee on Security Through Arms Control, and a technical report by WILLIAM C. DAVIDSON, MARVIN I. KALKSTEIN, and CHRISTOPH HOHENEMSER. Planning Pamphlet No. 108. Washington: National Planning Association, 1960.

New York Committee on Atomic Information. *Selected References on the Ethical Implications of Atomic Energy.* New York, 1948.

NIEBUHR, REINHOLD. *Christianity and Power Politics.* New York: Scribner, 1940.

————. *Christian Realism and Political Problems.* London: Faber & Faber, 1954.

————. *The Structure of Nations and Empires. A Study of the Recurring Patterns and Problems of the Political Order in Relation to the Unique Problems of the Nuclear Age.* New York: Scribner, 1959.

————. *Why the Christian Church is Not Pacifist.* London: Student Christian Movement Press, 1940.

————. *The World Crisis and American Responsibility.* Nine Essays; collected and edited by ERNEST W. LEFEVER. New York: Association, 1958.

ORR, EDGAR W. *Christian Pacifism.* Ashingdon, England: Daniel, 1958.

OSGOOD, ROBERT E. *Limited War. The Challenge to American Strategy.* Chicago: Univ. of Chicago Press, 1957.

PACHECO, JOSE DA SILVA. *O problema de guerra.* São Paulo: 1951.

PAULING, LINUS CARL. *No More War!* New York: Dodd, Mead, 1958.

PEETERS, PAUL. *Massive Retaliation. The Policy and its Critics,* Chicago: Regnery, 1959.

PIUS XII. *The Pope Speaks on Peace. Excerpts from Papal Pronouncements, 1944–1948.* Compiled by THOMAS P. NEILL. Washington: The Catholic Association for International Peace, 1949.

RAMSEY, PAUL. *Basic Christian Ethics.* New York: Scribner, 1950.

————. *War and the Christian Conscience.* Durham, N.C.: Duke University Press, to be published in 1961.

RICHTER, W. FRANZ. *The Atom Bomb! What it Really Means for Human Society.* London: Social Science Association, 1945.

ROBERTS, JOHN ERIC, and BELL, GEORGE. *Nuclear War and Peace, the Facts and the Challenge.* London: National Peace Council, 1955.

ROBINSON, GEORGE OSCAR. *And What of Tomorrow. The Human Drama in the Atomic Revolution and the Promise of a Golden Age.* New York: Comet, 1956.

Royal Institute of International Affairs. *On Limiting Atomic War.* London, New York: Royal Institute of International Affairs, 1956.

RYAN, JOHN KENNETH. *Modern War and Basic Ethics.* Milwaukee: Bruce, 1940.

St. John's University. *The Implications of Atomic Energy.* Five Essays on the scientific, sociological, legal, economic, and ethical implications of atomic energy. Brooklyn, N.Y.: St. John's Univ. Press, 1950.

SCHWARZENBERGER, GEORG. *The Legality of Nuclear Weapons.* London: Stevens, 1958.

SCHWEITZER, ALBERT. *Peace or Atomic War?* New York: Holt, 1958.
SHUB, ANATOLE (ed.). *Alternatives to the H-Bomb.* A Symposium Organized by The New Leader Magazine. Boston: Beacon, 1955.
SIBLEY, MULFORD Q. *The Political Theories of Modern Pacifism. An Analysis and Criticism.* Philadelphia: The Pacifist Research Bureau, 1944.
SIBLEY, MULFORD Q., and JACOB, PHILIP E. *Conscription of Conscience. The American State and the Conscientious Objector, 1940–1947.* Ithaca, N.Y.: Cornell Univ. Press, 1952.
SINGH, NAGENDRA. *Nuclear Weapons and International Law.* New York: Praeger, 1959.
SMITH, VINCENT EDWARD. *Footnotes for the Atom.* Milwaukee: Bruce, 1951.
SMITH, WILBUR MOOREHEAD. *This Atomic Age and the Word of God.* Boston: Wilde, 1948.
Social Science Research Council. Committee on Social and Economic Aspects of Atomic Energy. *Public Reaction to the Atomic Bomb and World Affairs. A Nation-Wide Survey of Attitudes and Information.* Ithaca, N.Y.: Cornell Univ. Press, 1947.
SPAIGHT, JAMES M. *The Atomic Problem.* London: A. Barron, 1948.
STRATMANN, FRANZISKUS M. *The Church and War.* New York: Kenedy, 1928.
———. *War and Christianity Today.* Westminster, Md.: Newman, 1956.
STRAUSZ-HUPE, ROBERT, with WILLIAM R. KINTNER, JAMES E. DOUGHERTY and ALVIN J. COTTRELL. *Protracted Conflict.* New York: Harper, 1959.
Symposium on Atomic Energy and its Implications. Philadelphia: The American Philosophical Society, 1946.
TAYLOR, MAXWELL D. *The Uncertain Trumpet.* New York: Harper, 1960.
TELLER, EDWARD, and LATTER, ALBERT L. *Our Nuclear Future. Facts, Dangers, and Opportunities.* New York: Criterion, 1958.
THOMPSON, CHARLES S. (ed.). *Morals and Missiles. Catholic Essays on the Problem of War Today.* London: James Clarke, 1959.
THOMPSON, KENNETH W. *Christian Ethics and the Dilemmas of Foreign Policy.* Published for the Lilly Endowment Research Program in Christianity and Politics. Durham, N.C.: Duke Univ. Press, 1959.
———. *Ethics and National Purpose.* New York: Church Peace Union, 1957.
———. *National Security and the Moral Problem.* New York: National Council of Churches, 1958.
———. *Political Realism and the Crisis of World Politics.* Princeton, N.J.: Princeton Univ. Press, 1960.
THOMPSON, REGINALD WILLIAM. *9 A.B.: The Challenge.* London: Spalding and Levy, 1953.
TOYNBEE, PHILIP. *The Fearful Choice. A Debate on Nuclear Policy.* London: Gollancz, 1958.
United States Atomic Energy Commission. *Civil Defense and Atomic Warfare. A Selected Reading List.* Washington: U.S. Government Printing Office, 1953.
United States Department of the Army. *Bibliography on Limited War.* Department of the Army Pamphlet No. 20–60. Washington: U.S. Government Printing Office, 1958.
United States Library of Congress. Legislative Reference Service. *Controlling the Further Development of Nuclear Weapons. A Collection of Excerpts and a Bibliography.* Washington: U.S. Government Printing Office, 1958.
United States Senate. Committee on Foreign Relations. *United States Foreign Policy: Developments in Military Technology and their Impact on United States Strategy and Foreign Policy.* A study prepared by the Washington

Center of Foreign Policy Research, The Johns Hopkins University. Committee Print. 86th Congress, 1st Session, December 6, 1959. Washington: U.S. Government Printing Office, 1959.

VANN, GERALD. *Morality and War*. London: Burns, Oates and Washbourne, 1939.

VEALE, FREDERICK J. P. *Advance to Barbarism*. Appleton, Wis.: C. C. Nelson, 1953.

WALCH, JOHN WESTON. *Debate Handbook on Nuclear Weapons*. Portland, Me., 1958.

————. *Supplement on Nuclear Weapons*. Portland, Me., 1959.

WALKER, SYDNOR HARBISON (ed.). *The First One Hundred Days of the Atomic Age, August 6–November 15, 1945*. Compilation of current opinion upon political and international implications of the Atomic bomb. New York: The Woodrow Wilson Foundation, 1946.

WALLACE, VICTOR HUGO (ed.). *Paths to Peace. A Study of War, its Causes and Prevention*. Carlton, Victoria: Melbourne Univ. Press, 1957.

WAYS, MAX. *Beyond Survival*. New York: Harper, 1959.

WENTWORTH, WILLIAM CHARLES. *Time and the Bomb. An Analysis of the Atomic Situation, s.l.*, 1953.

WHITE, VICTOR. *The Morality of War*. London: Blackfriars, 1949.

World Council of Churches. *Christians and the Prevention of War in an Atomic Age: a Theological Discussion*. Provisional Study Document issued by the Division of Studies by Action of the Central Committee of the World Council of Churches, August 27, 1958. New York: World Council of Churches, 1958.

————. *Peace is the Will of God. A Testimony of the World Council of Churches*. Statement prepared by the Historic Peace Churches and the International Fellowship of Reconciliation. New York: World Council of Churches, 1953.

WRIGHT, JOHN J. *Peace, the Work of Justice*. Washington: The Catholic Association for International Peace, 1958.

WUESTHOFF, FREDA. *There is no Time to Be Lost. Man in the Atomic Age*. Ravensburg: O. Maier, 1957.

YOUNG, WAYLAND HILTON. *Strategy for Survival*. Baltimore: Penguin, 1959.

III. Select continental publications

ANGELOPOULOS, ANGELOS. *L'atome unira-t-il le monde? Aspects économiques, sociaux, politiques*. Paris: R. Pichon and R. Durand–Auzias, 1956.

ARAGO, RICARDO. *Grandeza de Dios: El átomo*. Barcelona: Propaganda Católica, 1954.

Arbeitsgemeinschaft Sozialdemokratischer Akademiker. *Weltmacht Atom. Die atomaren Kräfte und ihre Auswirkungen auf des geistige, wirtschaftliche, militärische und politische Leben*. Frankfort/M.: Nest, 1955.

BAERWOLF, ADALBERT. *Il n'y a plus qu'à prier*. Translated from the German by J. BENOIST–MECHIN. Paris: A. Michel, 1958.

BARDELLINI, FILIPPO. *La bomba atomica e la potenza di Dio. Vi sono tanti esseri fuori di noi e più potenti di noi*. Vicenza: L. Favero, 1949.

BROCKMOELLER, KLEMENS. *Christentum am Morgen des Atomzeitalters*. 6th (unrevised) ed. Frankfort/M.: Knecht, 1955.

BUECHEL, WOLFGANG. "Raketen-Perspektiven," *Stimmen der Zeit* (Freiburg-i-Br.), 161 (March, 1958), 461–65.

Deutsche Gesellschaft für Auswärtige Politik. Forschungsinstitut, Frankfurt am Main. *Deutsches und ausländisches Schrifttum zur Frage der Abrüstung,*

1945–1956; unter besonderer Berücksichtigung des Schrifttums zu den Problemen der Kernwaffen und der internationalen Kontrolle der Kernenergie. Frankfort/M.: Deutsche Gesellschaft für Auswärtige Politik. Forschungsinstitut, 1957.

Les enseignements pontificaux. La paix internationale. Vol. I, *La guerre moderne.* Paris: Desclée, 1956.

GOLLWITZER, HELMUT. *Die Christen und die Atomwaffen.* Munich: Kaiser, 1957.

———. *Die christliche Gemeinde in der politischen Welt.* Tübingen: Mohr, 1954.

GOLLWITZER, HELMUT, VOGEL, HEINRICH, and HEIDLER, FRITZ. *Christlicher Glaube und atomare Waffen.* Berlin: Evangelische, 1959.

GRANERO, J. M. "Sobre la moralidad de las guerras modernas," *Razón y fe* (Madrid), 145 (April, 1952), 341–60.

GUENTHOER, ANSELM. "Der Papst über den Krieg," *Benediktinische Monatschrift* (Beuron/Hohenzollern), 34 (1958), 279–86, 371–79.

GUNDLACH, GUSTAV. "Die Lehre Pius' XII. vom modernen Krieg," *Stimmen der Zeit* (Freiburg-i.-Br.), 164 (April, 1959), 1–14.

———. "Der Papst und der Krieg," *Stimmen der Zeit* (Freiburg-i.-Br.), 159 (February, 1957), 378–79.

HANSLIAN, RUDOLF. *Vom Gaskampf zum Atomkrieg. Die Entwicklung der wissenschaftlichen Waffen.* Stuttgart: Chemiker–Zeitung, 1951.

HERBRUEGGEN, HUBERTUS SCHULTE. "Atomkrieg und christliche Ethik," *Frankfurter Hefte* (Frankfort/M.), 13 (September–October, 1958), 605–12, 686–94.

HIRSCHMANN, JOHANNES. "Kann atomare Verteidigung sittlich gerechtfertigt sein?" *Stimmen der Zeit* (Freiburg-i.-Br.), 162 (July, 1958), 284–96.

———. "Zur Diskussion um die Wehrpflicht," *Stimmen der Zeit* (Freiburg-i.-Br.), 159 (December, 1956), 203–16.

IRLE, RENE. *La bombe atomique et l'Apocalypse.* Bordeaux: Feret, 1947.

JASPERS, KARL. *Die Atombombe und die Zukunft des Menschen. Politisches Bewusstsein in unserer Zeit.* Munich: Piper, 1958.

"Ein katholisches Wort zur atomaren Rüstung," *Herder-Korrespondenz* (Freiburg-i.-Br.), 12 (June, 1958), 395–97.

"Krieg und Frieden: Die XL. Soziale Woche Frankreichs." *Herder-Korrespondenz* (Freiburg-i.-Br.), 8 (October, 1953), 39–44.

LABARTHE, ANDRE. *Statu quo de la peur.* Paris: Défense de la France, 1946.

LORSON, PIERRE. *Un chrétien peut-il être objecteur de conscience?* Paris: Seuil, 1950.

———. *Défense de tuer.* Paris: Centurion, 1956.

———. *Symphonie pacifique. La paix individuelle, nationale, internationale.* Strasbourg: Le Roux, 1948.

MESSINEO, A. "La comunità internazionale e il diritto di guerra," *Civiltà cattolica* (Rome), 106 (January 1, 1955), 72–76.

MUSULIN, JANKO. "Pax atomica, zweite Phase," *Wort und Wahrheit* (Vienna), 11 (May, 1956), 329–32.

NEF, JOHN ULRIC. *La route de la guerre totale. Essai sur les relations entre la guerre et le progrès humain.* Paris: Colin, 1949.

PETERS, KARL. "Probleme der Atomaufrüstung," *Hochland* (Munich), 51 (October, 1958), 12–25.

PICHT, WERNER. "Vom künftigen deutschen Soldaten," *Wort und Wahrheit* (Vienna), 11 (1956), 5–28, 413–32, 573–97.

167

PRIBILLA, MAX. "Krieg, Wehrwille und Kriegsdienstverweigerung," *Stimmen der Zeit* (Freiburg-i.-Br.), 151 (January, 1953), 270–82.

REGAMEY, R. *Non-violence et amour des ennemis.* Paris: Saint-Jacques, 1956.

———. *Non-violence et conscience chrétienne.* Paris: Cerf, 1958.

ROSE, ULRICH DETLEV (ed.). *Die unheimlichen Waffen. Atomraketen über uns: Lenkwaffen, Raketengeschosse, Atombomben.* Munich-Lochhausen: Schild, 1957.

"Rüstung und Gewissen im Atomzeitalter," *Herder-Korrespondenz* (Freiburg-i.-Br.), 9 (August, 1958), 509–16.

SCHMIDTHUES, KARLHEINZ. "Atomwaffen und Gewissen," *Wort und Wahrheit* (Vienna), 13 (June–July, 1958), 405–24.

STEIGER, HEINHARD. "Christliche Politik und die Versuchung zur Gewalttätigkeit. Gedanken anlässlich der Predigt des Kardinals Ottaviani," *Hochland* (Munich), 52 (April, 1960), 360–67.

TEILHARD DE CHARDIN, PIERRE. "Quelques réflexions sur le retentissement spirituel de la bombe atomique," *Études* (Paris), 250 (September, 1946), 223–30.

THIELICKE, HELMUT. *Fragen des Christentums an die moderne Welt. Eine christliche Kulturkritik.* Geneva: Oikumene, 1945.

UHLIG, ARNO WERNER. *Atom. Angst oder Hoffnung? Die Lehren des ersten Atommanövers der Welt.* Munich. Isar, 1955.

"Um die Erlaubtheit des modernen Krieges," *Stimmen der Zeit* (Freiburg-i.-Br.), 155 (November, 1954), 139.

VAUSSARD, MAURICE. "L'Eglise Catholique, la guerre et la paix," *Nouvelle revue théologique* (Louvain), 75 (November, 1953), 951–64.

"Vernichtungskrieg und Christentum," *Hochland* (Munich), 50 (August, 1958), 599–600.

"Die Warnungen des Papstes vor den Atomversuchen," *Herder-Korrespondenz* (Freiburg-i.-Br.), 11 (July, 1957), 455.

"Die Wehrdienstpflicht im Atomzeitalter," *Herder-Korrespondenz* (Freiburg-i.-Br.), 9 (September, 1955), 560–68.

WEILGART, WOLFGANG J. *Was ist normal im Schatten der Atombombe? Zur Psychologie des Aggressionstriebes.* Vienna: Gerold, 1957.

WELTY, EBERHARD. "Ächtung des Atomkrieges," *Die neue Ordnung* (Cologne), 8 (1954), 129–41.

WINTER, ERNST KARL. "Atomkraft und Atompolitik," *Schweizer Rundschau* (Zurich), 55 (September, 1955), 292–302.

———. "Die Atomkraft und der Friedender Menschheit," *Die österreichische Furche* (Vienna), 10 (December 11, 1954), 4; (December 18, 1954), 4; December 25, 1954), 3–4.

———. *Christentum und Zivilisation.* Vienna: Amandus, 1956.

———. "Probleme der Atomzivilisation," *Die österreichische Furche* (Vienna), 12 (March 10, 1956), 3–4; (March 17, 1956), 3–4; (March 24, 1956), 5.

"Wissenschaft und Verantwortung," *Stimmen der Zeit* (Freiburg-i.-Br.), 154 (July, 1954), 298–99.

WITT, OTTO. *Christ und Kriegsdienst, vom hohen Beruf der Gemeinde Jesu in der Welt.* Stuttgart–Degerloch: Vita Nuova, 1948.

ZALBA, MARCELINO. "Guerra atomica y moral," *Ecclesia* (Madrid), 10 (March 4, 1950), 239–41.

ZUPI, SAVERIO. *Codice christiano della pace.* Rome: Catholic Book Agency, 1954.